Two Hearts, One Path

Navigating the Joys and Challenges of a Long-Lasting Relationship

Dr. Charlotte Brown

Contents

Acknowledgment

Writing a book on the topic of "Two Hearts, One Path: Navigating the Joys and Challenges of a Long-Lasting Relationship" has been a deeply fulfilling and rewarding endeavor. It is with immense gratitude and appreciation that I acknowledge the individuals and sources that have contributed to the creation of this work.

First and foremost, I express my heartfelt gratitude to the countless couples and individuals who have shared their stories, experiences, and wisdom with me. Your openness, vulnerability, and willingness to reflect on the intricacies of long-lasting relationships have been the inspiration behind this book. Your courage to navigate the challenges and cherish the joys has shed light on the profound nature of enduring love.

I extend my deepest appreciation to my family and loved ones for their unwavering support throughout this writing process. Your belief in me and your encouragement have been invaluable in bringing this book to life. Your love and understanding have provided the foundation from which I have embarked on this journey of exploring the complexities of relationships.

I would like to express my gratitude to the countless authors, researchers, and experts in the field of psychology and relationships whose work has informed and enriched this book. Your insights, studies, and theories have provided a solid framework upon which I have built my exploration. Your dedication to understanding the dynamics of long-lasting relationships has broadened my perspective and deepened my understanding.

I would like to acknowledge the guidance and expertise of my editor and the publishing team who have worked diligently to shape and refine this manuscript. Your keen eye, constructive feedback, and commitment to excellence have been instrumental in crafting a book that I am proud to present to the readers.

Finally, I want to extend my heartfelt appreciation to the readers who have embarked on this journey with me. It is my sincere hope that the insights, strategies, and reflections shared within these pages will resonate with you and provide valuable guidance in navigating the joys and challenges of your own long-lasting relationships. Your trust and engagement are truly cherished.

Writing this book has been a labor of love, and I am profoundly grateful for the support, guidance, and inspiration that have accompanied me on this transformative journey. May this work serve as a source of encouragement, growth, and connection for all who explore its pages.

With deepest gratitude

[Charlotte Brown]

Introduction

Love is a remarkable force that brings two hearts together and places them on a path that is full of opportunities, possibilities, challenges, and joys. When two people decide to be in a long lasting relationship, their lives become intertwined and they embark on a life changing journey that has a profound impact on their futures. "Two Hearts One path: Navigating the Joys and Challenges of a Long Lasting Relationship" is a sincere look at the difficulties of maintaining a love that endures.

In this book, we dive into the embroidery of a dependable relationship, where the strings of dedication, trust, and flexibility are woven. We comprehend that relationships are not static; they require continuous consideration, attention, ongoing care and a common obligation to development and growth. Whether you are embarking on a new relationship or have been strolling this way for a really long time, this book fills in as a directing buddy and guiding companion, offering bits of knowledge and useful insight to explore the delights and difficulties that come your direction.

Within these pages, you will find the significance of building a solid foundation, where trust and open communication become the bedrock of your relationship. We investigate the sensitive harmony among independence and fellowship, understanding that while two hearts thump as one, every heart merits its own space to prosper. Embracing emotional intimacy turns into a fundamental part of your excursion, as you develop your association and really grasp the internal functions of your partner's heart.

We likewise perceive that tempests will emerge en route, testing the strength of your bond. Together, we will investigate methodologies to explore clashes with effortlessness, to encourage backing and cooperation during testing times, and to set out on the excursion of forgiveness and healing when wounds arise. Through shared weakness and a pledge to development, you will find that difficulties can be changed into open doors for more profound connection and understanding.

However, this book isn't just about beating hindrances and overcoming obstacles; it is tied in with sustaining a thriving and flourishing partnership. We praise the delights of development, the power of romance and the craft of setting shared dreams. We explore the excellence of growing together, persistently rediscovering each other, and developing an affection that flourishes in the midst of the recurring pattern of life.

All through these pages, you will track down practical direction, genuine stories, and interesting activities that support thoughtfulness and significant conversation. As you set out on this excursion, I welcome you to consider your own encounters, expectations, and dreams. Together, we will explore the intricacies of affection and love drawing motivation and inspiration from the accounts of couples who have set out on this way before us.

"Two Hearts, One path: Exploring the Delights and Difficulties of a Dependable Relationship" is a tribute and ode to the groundbreaking power of love, a recognition for the versatile hearts that challenge to walk together, connected at the hip, down the twisting way of life. Thus, let us set out on this excursion together, with open hearts and receptive outlooks, prepared to embrace the endowment of an enduring relationship.

Embarking on a Journey of Love and Commitment" explores the profound and transformative experience of entering into a long-lasting relationship filled with love, dedication, and unwavering commitment. It delves into the essence of embarking on this extraordinary journey, highlighting the joys, challenges, and rewards that come with choosing to embark on a path of love and lifelong partnership.

When two hearts come together in a deep and meaningful way, a journey begins an adventure filled with excitement, growth, and shared experiences. This exploration dives into the essence of love and commitment, shedding light on the intricacies and complexities that accompany the decision to embark on this journey with another person.

Embarking on a journey of love and commitment requires a solid foundation rooted in trust, open communication, and mutual respect. It involves making a conscious choice to prioritize the well-being and happiness of both partners, nurturing a deep connection that withstands the tests of time.

This exploration invites individuals to reflect on their personal motivations and desires as they embark on this journey. It encourages self-awareness, as individuals recognize their own needs, values, and aspirations, and how these align with those of their partner. It emphasizes the importance of clear and honest communication, creating a shared vision, and setting mutual goals that serve as guiding stars throughout the journey.

As with any journey, challenges may arise along the way. This exploration acknowledges the obstacles that couples may encounter and provides guidance on navigating them with grace and resilience. It explores strategies for effective conflict resolution, fostering understanding and empathy, and nurturing emotional intimacy. It highlights the power of support and teamwork in overcoming obstacles, reminding couples that they are stronger together.

But beyond the challenges lie countless moments of joy, growth, and fulfillment. This exploration celebrates the small victories, the shared laughter, and the deep connection that can be found in the everyday moments. It encourages couples to savor the journey, appreciating the beauty in the simplest of things and finding solace in the love and commitment they share.

Embarking on a journey of love and commitment is a transformative experience that calls for courage, vulnerability, and unwavering dedication. It is a journey of self-discovery, personal growth, and the profound joy of walking hand in hand with a loved one. It is a journey that holds the potential for deep connection, lifelong companionship, and a love story that defies the boundaries of time.

Embarking on a journey of love and commitment is an extraordinary undertaking that holds immeasurable rewards. It requires trust, open communication, and mutual support. By embracing the challenges, celebrating the victories, and nurturing the love and commitment shared, individuals can embark on a journey that fills their lives with joy, meaning, and an everlasting bond.

Part I

Laying the Foundation

Chapter 1

Building a Solid Foundation: The Power of Trust and Communication

In any enduring relationship, a solid foundation is the bedrock upon which love and commitment flourish. It is through trust and open communication that two hearts forge a deep connection and build a lasting bond. In this chapter, "Building a So
lid Foundation: The Power of Trust and Communication," we delve into the fundamental pillars that sustain a long-lasting relationship.

Trust forms the cornerstone of every successful partnership. It is the unwavering belief in each other's reliability, honesty, and integrity. Trust allows us to let go of doubts and insecurities, knowing that our partner's actions and words align with their intentions. It creates a safe space where vulnerability can thrive, nurturing a deep sense of emotional intimacy. Throughout the pages that follow, we will explore ways to establish, nurture, and rebuild trust, recognizing that it requires consistent effort and a commitment to open-heartedness.

Communication, on the other hand, serves as the lifeblood of any relationship. It is the means by which we connect, understand, and share our innermost thoughts and feelings. Effective communication transcends mere words, encompassing active listening, empathy, and the ability to express ourselves authentically. We will uncover valuable tools and strategies to enhance communication within your relationship, fostering understanding, resolving conflicts, and nurturing a culture of open and honest dialogue.

In the exploration of trust and communication, we recognize that no two relationships are the same. Each couple has their own unique dynamics, histories, and challenges. However, the principles and insights shared within these pages are universal, offering guidance that can be applied to any partnership.

As you embark on this journey of building a solid foundation, I encourage you to reflect on your own experiences, strengths, and areas for growth. Consider the dynamics of trust within your relationship – the moments that have strengthened it and the times when it may have been tested. Reflect on the patterns of communication between you and your partner, recognizing areas where improvements can be made and celebrating the moments of deep connection and understanding.

Building a solid foundation is not a one-time endeavor but a continuous process that evolves and adapts as you and your partner grow together. Through introspection, open-hearted conversations, and a willingness to learn, you will uncover the transformative power of trust and communication, paving the way for a resilient and fulfilling partnership.

So, let us embark on this chapter together, with an open mind and a commitment to growth. As we explore the power of trust and communication, may it deepen your understanding of yourself and your partner, fostering a connection that withstands the test of time.

The topic of "Building a Solid Foundation: The Power of Trust and Communication" delves into the fundamental pillars that form the bedrock of a healthy and successful relationship. Trust and communication are essential components that contribute to the strength, longevity, and overall satisfaction of a partnership.

This extensive exploration aims to shed light on the profound impact of trust and communication in relationships and provide insights, strategies, and practical tools to cultivate these crucial elements. It recognizes that trust and communication are intertwined, with each reinforcing and supporting the other, and that they are essential for establishing and maintaining a solid foundation.

Trust is the cornerstone of any successful relationship. It is the belief, confidence, and reliance on the integrity, character, and actions of one's partner. Trust involves vulnerability and the willingness to open oneself up to the possibility of being hurt, while having faith in the commitment, loyalty, and honesty of the other person. Building trust requires consistency, transparency, and accountability, and it is nurtured through acts of reliability, respect, and emotional support.

Communication serves as the lifeblood of a relationship, allowing for the exchange of thoughts, feelings, desires, and needs. Effective communication involves active listening, expressing oneself clearly and honestly, and fostering an atmosphere of openness and understanding. It encompasses both verbal and non-verbal cues, as well as the ability to empathize and validate the experiences and perspectives of one's partner. Communication lays the foundation for intimacy, connection, and conflict resolution.

The exploration highlights the transformative power of trust and communication in relationships. It emphasizes that trust and communication serve as buffers during challenging times, fostering resilience and providing a sense of security. Trust allows partners to rely on each other's support, knowing that they have each other's best interests at heart. Effective communication ensures that both partners feel heard, understood, and valued, leading to a deeper emotional connection.

Furthermore, the exploration offers practical strategies and tools to cultivate trust and improve communication within a relationship. It encourages individuals to foster self-awareness, develop active listening skills, and practice empathy. It explores the importance of setting boundaries, managing conflicts constructively, and nurturing a culture of openness and honesty.

At last, building a solid foundation through trust and communication is an ongoing process that requires commitment, effort, and dedication from both partners. It involves continuous learning, growth, and adaptation as the relationship evolves over time. By prioritizing trust and communication, individuals can foster a safe and supportive environment that nurtures love, intimacy, and long-term satisfaction.

All things considered, the power of trust and communication cannot be overstated in the context of building a solid foundation for a successful relationship. Trust lays the groundwork for vulnerability and emotional connection, while communication ensures that both partners feel heard, understood, and valued. By cultivating trust and fostering effective communication, individuals can create a resilient and fulfilling partnership that stands the test of time.

Chapter 2

Honoring Individuality: Balancing Independence and Togetherness

In the unpredictable dance of a Long lasting relationship, there exists a fragile harmony between honoring individuality or respecting uniqueness and embracing the quintessence of togetherness. A dance commends the interesting characters, yearnings, and necessities of each partner while supporting the profound bond that joins them. In this section, "Respecting Distinction: Adjusting Freedom and Harmony," or "Honoring Individuality: Balancing Independence and Togetherness," we embark on a profound exploration of the craft of harmonizing personal awareness, growth and shared connection inside a serious and committed relationship.

At the core of honoring individuality and respecting independence lies the significant acknowledgment that every individual brings a particular arrangement of encounters, yearnings, and interests to the relationship. It is a challenge to celebrate and support the complex perspectives that make each couple what their identity is. Respecting singularity and honoring individuality implies giving the opportunity and space for self-improvement, self discovery, and the quest for individual dreams. Through this development of singularity each accomplice carries their genuine self to the relationship, contributing their special viewpoints, gifts, and interests.

At the center of each and every persevering through partnership is the acknowledgment and festivity of every individual's particular character. It is an affirmation that while two hearts thump or beat as one, they hold their own interests, passion, and dreams. Respecting uniqueness or Honoring individuality implies cultivating a climate that supports personal growth and self discovery. Through this cycle each partner carries their valid self to the relationship, contributing remarkable points of view, qualities, and yearnings. In the pages ahead, we will dig into the significance of safeguarding distinction or preserving individuality looking at how it upgrades the lavishness and richness of a relationship and considers the spreading out of personal potential.

Balancing independence and togetherness is a dynamic dance, and require a delicate interplay of understanding, respect, grace, and effective communication. It is a delicate harmony that respects and supports each partner's need for autonomy, while fostering a deep sense of connection and interdependence. Striking this delicate balance entails creating an environment that allows each partner to pursue personal interests, goals, and self-care, while maintaining an unwavering commitment to the shared journey of love and growth. Throughout this chapter, we will explore practical strategies, insights, and reflective exercises that encourage open and compassionate dialogue, helping partners navigate the complexities of balancing individuality and togetherness.

Moreover, the art of honoring individuality and embracing togetherness extends beyond external pursuits. It encompasses the emotional landscape, the nurturing of inner worlds, and the preservation of self while embarking on the shared path of love. By allowing each partner to maintain their unique identity, dreams, and personal growth, the relationship becomes a catalyst for mutual flourishing, offering a supportive and empowering environment that propels both partners to new heights of self-awareness, fulfillment, and authenticity.

As you engage with this chapter, take a moment to reflect on your own relationship. Consider the ways in which you and your partner honor and encourage each other's individuality. Reflect on the delicate balance between independence and togetherness within your partnership, and explore areas where growth, understanding, and adjustments may be necessary. This chapter offers a transformative opportunity to deepen your understanding of the dance between honoring individuality and embracing togetherness, providing insights, tools, and perspectives that will enrich and strengthen the unique tapestry of your relationship.

Finding equilibrium between honoring individuality and embracing togetherness is a continuous journey, one that evolves and unfolds as each partner grows and evolves. The pages that follow will illuminate the transformative power of fostering personal growth and embracing the beauty of shared connection within the context of a committed relationship. It is a journey that opens the doors to deeper intimacy, mutual support, and a love that thrives on the authenticity and empowerment of each partner.

So, let us embark on this exploration together, with open hearts and open minds, ready to celebrate the mosaic of individuality and the symphony of togetherness. May this chapter guide you in navigating the delicate balance, fostering an environment where both partners can shine brightly as they embark on the journey of love and personal growth, hand in hand.

The topic of "Honoring Individuality: Balancing Independence and Togetherness" delves into the delicate dance between maintaining one's sense of self while being in a committed partnership.

It recognizes the importance of honoring and nurturing the individuality of each partner while simultaneously fostering a strong and meaningful connection as a couple.

This comprehensive exploration aims to shed light on the significance of striking a balance between independence and togetherness in a relationship. It recognizes that each partner brings unique strengths, interests, and aspirations to the partnership and that honoring individuality is essential for personal growth, fulfillment, and the overall health of the relationship.

Honoring individuality involves acknowledging and celebrating the distinct identities, dreams, and values of each partner. It embraces the understanding that while a relationship brings two individuals together, it should not diminish or overshadow their individuality. Instead, it encourages the cultivation of personal passions, pursuits, and self-care as essential ingredients for a thriving partnership.

Balancing independence and togetherness requires open and honest communication between partners. It involves active listening, empathy, and a genuine interest in understanding and supporting each other's individual needs and aspirations. It entails creating space for personal growth and self-expression while fostering a deep emotional connection and shared goals as a couple.

The exploration highlights the transformative power of honoring individuality and balancing independence and togetherness in relationships. It recognizes that when both partners feel supported and encouraged to pursue their individual passions and interests, it enhances self-esteem, satisfaction, and overall relationship quality. By maintaining a strong sense of self, individuals bring unique perspectives, strengths, and experiences that enrich the partnership.

Furthermore, the exploration offers practical strategies and insights to navigate the delicate balance between independence and togetherness. It encourages partners to engage in open and non-judgmental conversations about personal boundaries, goals, and needs. It explores the importance of fostering trust, respect, and mutual support, which allows each partner to thrive individually and as a couple.

Keeping up with distinction is basic to establishing sound and healthy organization. As a result, maintaining a healthy relationship and taking care of oneself must be prioritized equally. Taking a trip down memory lane to recall our early childhood bonds is the first step in understanding how we maintain our individual identities while building our partnership. It was during this time that we developed our sense of identity and our capacity to form healthy connections with other people. We learn to see our mother as both a separate person with whom we can empathize and a caretaker on whom we rely because of her unwavering support of our growing independence. Every human connection is based on this foundation of independence and dependence. However, dependency issues later on in romantic relationships can result from impeded or subparts independent development in childhood. One might look to their partner to bolster their identity rather than having a strong sense of self.

To be a superior individual in your life and a decent partner in your relationship, it's important that you endeavor to keep areas of strength for freedom and independence and an advanced perspective. With this continuous objective, you can proceed to develop and reinforce your extraordinary attributes as well as conduct that mirrors your inclinations and beliefs. In your relationship, you should be cautious that you are not searching for somebody to finish your deficiency or to characterize or attest you.

Be grown up. It's normal for individuals to whine of their partners being juvenile and declining to grow up. Being grown up isn't simply an issue of a sincerely mature way of behaving. Being genuinely grown up likewise includes perceiving your youth's injury and misfortunes, doing whatever it takes to determine them, and understanding how they helped shape your ongoing way of behaving. It implies effectively distinguishing and testing the safeguards you framed as a kid and revising the negative perspectives or inclinations you procured.

Be open and undefended. Receptiveness includes the capacity to be blunt in uncovering and communicating your own sentiments, contemplations, dreams, and wants. Being nondefensive and open to criticism is one of the most significant relationship abilities you can create. Rather than protecting yourself from your partner's reactions or ideas, you can search for the bit of truth in what your partner is talking about, in light of the fact that it might offer you a chance for self-improvement. At the point when you're worried in this manner with your improvement as an individual, you can stay open to change in your personal connection yet additionally hold your healthy identity, your solidarity, and your uniqueness.

Being straightforward is fundamental to your respectability as an individual, and important to the improvement of confidence in your cozy relationship. It's ideal to be straightforward in any event, when it is difficult to come clean. At the point when you are underhanded or straightforwardly untruthful with your partner, you deceive yourself, and you crack your partner's feeling of the real world. You likewise harm the trust and closeness between you. Love requires truth in light of the fact that without truth you can't assemble and keep up with the trust that is vital for a close connection.

Regard your partner by empowering your partner's remarkable advantages and individual objectives, autonomous of your own. Be delicate to your partner's needs, wants, and sentiments, and put as much worth on them as you do all alone. This sort of interest in and feeling for your partner is philanthropic and goes past any narrow minded or self service concerns you might have.

To accomplish this degree of respect, you want to have sympathy with and empathy for your partner. This includes involving your brain as well as your feelings and instinct to see and vicariously experience the idea of your adored one. At the point when you comprehend your partner in this profoundly compassionate way, you know about what you share practically speaking, however you likewise perceive and esteem your disparities and differences.

Eventually, honoring individuality and finding a balance between independence and togetherness is a dynamic and ongoing process within a relationship. It requires a commitment to personal growth, self-reflection, and open-mindedness. By valuing and nurturing the individuality of each partner, couples can cultivate a strong foundation that supports personal fulfillment and a deep, meaningful connection.

Taking everything into account, honoring individuality and balancing independence and togetherness are vital components of a healthy and fulfilling relationship. By embracing and supporting each other's individuality, couples can create an environment that encourages personal growth, self-expression, and mutual respect. The ability to strike a harmonious balance between independence and togetherness allows for a partnership that thrives on both individual strengths and shared goals, ultimately fostering a deep and lasting connection.

Chapter 3

Nurturing Emotional Intimacy: Deepening the Connection

Emotional intimacy is the sacred ground on which two souls connect and become intertwined in a long-term relationship. It is the deep and genuine bond that goes beyond the physical and into the heart's depths. In this part, "Nurturing Emotional Intimacy: Deepening the Connection," we begin a life-altering investigation into the art of fostering emotional closeness, fostering vulnerability, and cultivating the sacred connection that is at the heart of a committed partnership.

Emotional intimacy is the foundation whereupon love flourishes and twists. It is the ability to be completely seen, comprehended, and acknowledged by our partner as well as to offer something very similar to them. It is a space where weaknesses are shared, fears are mitigated, and dreams are upheld. Through emotional intimacy, the obstructions that different us break down, making a safe haven of trust, sympathy, and profound understanding. In the pages that follow, we will dive into the significant meaning of sustaining emotional intimacy, exploring the practices, bits of knowledge, and devices that consider its continuous growth and extending.

Developing emotional intimacy requires a cognizant obligation to develop key components that cultivate connections and weakness. Trust shapes the underpinning of emotional intimacy giving a place of refuge where the two partners have a solid sense of safety in sharing their most valid selves. It is through belief that we can open our hearts, permitting our partner's to observe the unguarded snapshots of our lives and giving the space to them to do likewise. Weakness, as well, is fundamental, as it is the eagerness to uncover our apprehensions, instabilities, and most profound feelings without reservation, realizing that we will be met with empathy and understanding.

Throughout this chapter, we will explore practical strategies and exercises to nurture emotional intimacy within your relationship. We will delve into the power of active listening, emotional attunement, and non-verbal cues that deepen understanding and strengthen the emotional bond. We will also examine the role of self-reflection and self-awareness in fostering emotional intimacy, recognizing that our ability to connect deeply with our partner is rooted in our own understanding and acceptance of our emotions.

As you engage with this chapter, take a moment to reflect on your own relationship and the level of emotional intimacy you have cultivated. Consider the moments that have deepened your connection and the challenges that may have hindered its growth. Reflect on the patterns of communication and the ways in which you can create a safe and nurturing environment for emotional vulnerability to thrive. This chapter offers an opportunity for self-discovery and growth, providing insights and practical tools to cultivate a deeper emotional connection with your partner.

Nurturing emotional intimacy is an ongoing journey, one that requires patience, vulnerability, and a commitment to growth. The following pages will illuminate the transformative power of emotional closeness, revealing its ability to create a love that is nourished by deep understanding, compassion, and authenticity.

So, let us embark on this exploration together, with open hearts and open minds, ready to embrace the transformative power of nurturing emotional intimacy. May this chapter guide you in deepening the sacred bond with your partner, fostering a connection that transcends the mundane and thrives on the profound and authentic exchange of hearts. Or flourishes in the depths of your shared emotions and understanding.

The topic of "Nurturing Emotional Intimacy: Deepening the Connection" explores the profound and transformative nature of emotional intimacy within a relationship. It delves into the essential components that contribute to deepening the emotional connection between partners and offers insights, strategies, and practical tools to nurture and strengthen this aspect of the relationship.

Emotional intimacy refers to the deep sense of closeness, trust, and vulnerability that partners share with one another. It involves the ability to express and understand one's own emotions, as well as to empathize and connect with the emotions of the partner. Nurturing emotional intimacy requires creating a safe and supportive space where both partners can openly share their thoughts, feelings, fears, and desires without judgment or criticism.

This comprehensive exploration highlights the significance of emotional intimacy as the foundation for a strong and fulfilling relationship. It recognizes that emotional intimacy fosters trust, empathy, and understanding, allowing partners to feel truly seen, heard, and accepted. Deepening the emotional connection enhances the bond between partners and creates a sense of security, belonging, and emotional support.

Nurturing emotional intimacy involves various practices and principles. It emphasizes the importance of active listening, where partners genuinely pay attention to one another's words, body language, and emotions. It encourages validation and empathy, where partners seek to understand and acknowledge each other's experiences and emotions, fostering a sense of emotional validation and connection.

The exploration also highlights the role of self-awareness and self-reflection in nurturing emotional intimacy. It encourages individuals to explore and understand their own emotions, needs, and triggers, allowing for greater vulnerability and authentic sharing with their partner. By cultivating self-awareness, individuals can communicate their emotional experiences more effectively and create a deeper connection with their partner.

Furthermore, the exploration delves into the power of emotional attunement and responsiveness in nurturing emotional intimacy. It explores the importance of being attuned to each other's emotional cues and needs, and the significance of responding with empathy, compassion, and support. It emphasizes the value of creating rituals of connection, such as regular check-ins, quality time together, and shared experiences, to foster emotional intimacy.

Effective communication fills in as the scaffold that traverses the abyss of emotional distance, empowering partners to communicate their sentiments, needs, and wants with lucidity and sympathy. It is the specialty of undivided attention, of really hearing and figuring out our partner's viewpoint, and answering with consideration and regard. Through legitimate and open communication, emotional intimacy is supported and extended, making a space where the two partner's feel seen, heard, and esteemed.

Being in a healthy, sincerely developed, emotionally mature, personal connection and intimate relationship is something that the vast majority try to experience. I characterizes intimacy as "an individual's capacity to connect with one more person on a profound, individual level." This is accomplished when the two individuals feel engaged to be their actual selves through a solid feeling of association, common regard, and veritable love.

The truth, notwithstanding, of how to build a solid, intimate relationships can be challenging. This is particularly evident on the off chance that the two individuals are muddled about — and not in total agreement about — the shared objectives they could each profit from in this optimal partnershipHi. An additional test would be on the off chance that a relationship has degenerated into a hazardous and poisonous one. For this situation, the work expected to retouch the relationship and mend any injuries could need proficient support.

Fortunately there are numerous things you can do to make a dependable, cherishing, intimate relationship.

I offers you 10 straightforward yet powerful ways you can encourage intimacy and revive the delight in your relationship.

1. Find Things You Share Practically Speaking

An amazing method for making more intimacy is to share exercises you both appreciate. Sharing forms intimacy and keeps you searching for what functions admirably between you. Cultivating a feeling of tomfoolery and good cheer in any relationship is significant.

Find the delight you can share together, even in the easily overlooked details. It doesn't need to be a major excursion or costly occasion to make it exceptional. An excursion, a twilight walk, a beautiful drive, watching the dawn, or attempting another recipe together are only a couple of instances of straightforward shared exercises that can make enduring intimacy. Explore new parts of life that unite you and you will feel the closeness you long to have.

2. Assume The Best About One Another

In the event that there is an example of a harmful way of behaving from your partner, expecting the most terrible things about them can be testing not. As opposed to presuming that your partner is deliberately attempting to be pernicious, take a full breath and assume the best about your partner that they were to be sure not to be mindful of their frightful way of behaving or words. This will go quite far in keeping the relationship sound, mature, and associated. It will likewise remake the trust expected to feel like you have each other's back.

3. Keep Away From Correlations

Your relationship is one of a kind. Try not to contrast it with others. Tune into the uniqueness of the bond you have with your partner. Your association and connection with your partner will appear to be unique than any other individual's. Try not to balance your relationship with your folks' relationship, or your previous relationship with a secondary school darling. It won't resemble your dearest spouse relationship with their partner or what you read last week about connections in a magazine. Be careful not to transform different connections that you see into principles. Assuming that you do this, you are unwittingly setting up bogus assumptions and worsening contrasts you have with your partner, which can toss the relationship out of equilibrium. Embrace your unmistakable relationship dynamic and all the excellence it offers.

4. Convey Genuinely and Deferentially

Accusing, judging, or condemning your partner isn't being aware. On the other hand, talking your reality in a careful and pleasant way implies you dare to tell your partner that you are harmed, frightened, irate, miserable, or humiliated by anything collaboration occurred. A basic method for accomplishing this is by utilizing "I" proclamations that express the thing you are feeling and why, which kills protectiveness in your partner. For instance, "I felt disheartened and furious when our supper time understanding was not satisfied" is coming from an enabled and harmless spot. Versus "I'm irate with you for being late to supper," which is accusing and impairs the two individuals. At the point when you talk your reality, it implies you are able to gallantly walk your discussion by completely finishing the arrangements you've made together. Being powerless and uncovering your sentiments to your partner is the endowment of legit communication and trust that fortifies the underpinning of a relationship.

5. Characterize What An Equivalent Partnership Resembles

Having a legit discussion and settling on arrangements about one another's vision of what an equivalent relationship feels like assists with making and keep up with that fairness. This incorporates how to offer thanks to one another and how to approach each other with deference, graciousness, and sympathy. At the point when this is polished, it makes a Relationship of Equivalents. There are no twofold principles, i.e., you hold yourself to a similar norm to which you hold your partner. Every individual's voice has a similar weight and worth. There is common help for one another's need to develop. There is likewise a work and eagerness to think and act more like a "we" as a method for offsetting the manners in which you as of now suspect and carry on like a "me." An equivalent relationship works more like a grown up to grown up trade as opposed to like a parent to kid dynamic. A valuable activity is to together work out a meaning of an equivalent partnership and incorporate the points of interest of what you concur upon. This is an extraordinary device to get clearness and straightforwardness and a superb update when you might arrive at an obstacle.

6. Check in With Your Partner Intermittently

Having customary check in helps keep a decent relationship moving in a healthy and agreeable heading. It's perfect to do this as a feature of a night out and energizes proceeded with real communication. It is likewise vital to track down ways of doing this in little ways consistently, maybe over breakfast or by the day's end before rest. Be inventive and find what works for you both. You might see a shared softness and expanded reverence for the additional communication.

7. Minimize Contrasts

External dissension can frequently cause us to feel like the relationship is ill fated. We will generally twist and succumb to the misrepresented rendition we tell ourselves attributable to our emotional injuries. All things considered, deliberately put away what has all the earmarks of being disagreement on a superficial level and listen profoundly for the tones that are bringing together and agreeable. This requires some work on the grounds that the hints of the previous contention might in any case ring noisily in our ears and stinging us. Relinquish your understanding and on second thought trust there is a more profound connection that is calling.

8. Pose Explaining Inquiries

Once in a while let an individual know that comprehending their perspective isn't enough since what they have communicated is truly stowing away at a more profound level. Posing a few explaining inquiries is better. This is useful because of multiple factors. In the first place, it assists them with realizing you are sincerely attempting to comprehend. Second, it assists you with trying not to accept what you do. Finally, it assists your join forces with going further into their sentiments so they can communicate with them better. You can say, "Assuming I see accurately, you feel this… . therefore. Is that right?" Truly getting to the central issue is recuperating and can assist with keeping away from miscommunication and conceivably put you in a terrible mood.

9. Foster Emotional Intimacy Through Capacity to Understand Anyone on a Deeper Level

The ability to appreciate individuals on a profound level alludes to having a familiarity with the emotional excursion you have been on that has formed your character. That emotional range should incorporate both the light side and the clouded side of your encounters. Alongside monitoring what causes you to feel adored, blissful, enthusiastic, bold, thankful, and euphoric, you should likewise have a comprehension of what causes you to feel terrified, hurt, irate, miserable, and embarrassed. Having this expansive profound information on yourself empowers you to: a) have sympathy and compassion for other people, b) make it feasible for you to pardon others and yourself, and c) make a more profound emotional connection with the individual you love by being genuinely open to them.

10. Pay Attention To Fundamental Vibrations

We frequently take the expressions of our partners in a real sense. Indeed, even in circumstances where your partner is a decent communicator, pay attention to what your partner is talking about past the words. Vibrational attunement with your partner holds the way to extraordinary communication. Address the strict particulars when you answer, however more critically address what is truly being partaken in the implicit domain. Utilize your creative mind and instinct — two basic apparatuses that can uncover further messages. Feel into your partner's quintessence and sense what it is they are feeling. Try not to constantly race to fix things, just be. This will open up ways to a more profound, more extravagant relationship.

You and your companion have a decent marriage-incredible, even-yet you're prepared to take it to a higher level. Perhaps you're actually cozy and physically intimate, however you believe a greater amount of that intimacy should reach out to your emotional life.

In this present chapter, we're sharing five ways to build the emotional intimacy in your relationship. Every one of these tips expands on the close to assist you with making the profound, satisfying connection you're desiring.

SUSTAIN TRUST

For your union with be essentially as genuinely private as could really be expected, you and your life partner should have the option to trust each other certainly. This implies that both of you should focus on continuously being straightforward with each other, talking reality in affection.

It likewise implies that you ought to demonstrate reliability for your spouse. In the event that your better half or spouse notices you being deceptive with an outsider under any circumstance you've sowed a seed of uncertainty in their heart. It's extremely challenging to conquer breaks in trust, so give a valiant effort to try not to make pointless issues.

GUARANTEE EMOTIONAL SECURITY

As well as being reliable, you and your spouse can build your intimacy by promising each other emotional security in your relationship. Affectionately tolerating your life partner, imperfections and everything, is a definitive presentation of affection and a contribution of wellbeing.

If neither of you needs to stress over being wrongly judged, condemned, or cut down, you will both flourish!

ENERGIZE WEAKNESS

With the endowment of emotional security comes the challenge to be defenseless. Permitting yourselves to be valid with each other will add a more profound layer of closeness to your marriage. As you find an opportunity to acknowledge your spouse's weaknesses, yet in addition uncover your own, your adoration for each other will become further.

Nobody on earth will know you in the manner in which your spouse knows you. What's more, nobody will realize your mate as you do. The most effective way to arrive is to be who you are with each other without affection and pretense.

DEVELOP CLOSENESS

Getting to know each other and sharing exercises will give you the actual closeness you really want to support your sentiment, as well as your fellowship. Regardless of whether you're short on extra energy, try to contribute essentially a couple of moments daily up close and personal, appreciating each other's conversation. The more associated you feel, the more cozy and intimate your marriage will be!

CULTIVATE PROFOUND CONNECTION

Feeling significantly associated with your spouse can influence both of you (decidedly!) on a profound and spiritual level, notwithstanding the advantages you'll feel genuinely and truly. Carve out opportunities to find out about each other. Assuming there's something your mate feels enthusiastically about, pose inquiries to find out more. Or on the other hand in the event that they love or appreciate something profoundly, show interest in it.

Interface where you are capable, whether or not you have similar arrangement of interests.

Settling on something worth agreeing on together and delighting in that as opposed to zeroing in on regions where you disagree or impact each other will soar your close to home closeness and emotional intimacy.

At last, nurturing emotional intimacy and deepening the connection is a continual and intentional process within a relationship. It requires ongoing effort, communication, and vulnerability from both partners. By cultivating emotional safety, active listening, empathy, and responsiveness, couples can create an environment that encourages emotional intimacy and strengthens the bond between them.

Taking everything into account, nurturing emotional intimacy and deepening the connection is a vital aspect of a fulfilling and meaningful relationship. It forms the foundation for trust, empathy, and understanding between partners. By prioritizing emotional intimacy and practicing the principles and strategies outlined in this exploration, couples can foster a deep, authentic, and lasting connection that enhances their overall well-being and satisfaction in the relationship.

Part II

Weathering the Storm

Chapter 4

Resolving Conflict with Grace: Strategies for Effective Communication

In the embroidery of an enduring long lasting relationship, clashes, disagreement and conflicts are an unavoidable piece of the excursion. Nonetheless, how we explore and determine these struggles has the ability to shape the course of our romantic tale. In this section, "Resolving Conflict with Grace: Strategies for Effective Communication," we leave on an extraordinary investigation of the craft of compromise, finding the significant effect that compelling communication can have on the wellbeing and life span of a serious partnership.

Conflict is certainly not an indication of shortcoming or disappointment but instead a chance for development, growth and understanding. When drawn nearer with beauty and a goal to find resolution, conflicts can develop our connection, reinforce our bond, and lead to more noteworthy emotional intimacy. Settling conflicts with beauty requires the development of powerful relational abilities, empathy, and an eagerness to comprehend and approve each other's points of view. In the pages that follow, we will delve into the meaning of excelling at compromise, remembering it as a foundation of a flourishing and amicable and harmonious relationship.

Viable communication lies at the core of compromise, offering the apparatuses and methodologies important to explore troublesome discussions with sympathy and understanding. Through transparent discourse, partner's can communicate their sentiments, needs, and worries, while effectively paying attention to their partner's point of view. Compelling communication empowers us to uncover the basic reasons for struggle and conflicts, find shared views, and work together to track down commonly helpful arrangements.

Inside the domain of conflicts resolution, moving toward conversations with beauty and empathy is fundamental. This implies rehearsing undivided attention, looking to comprehend prior to trying to be perceived. It implies perceiving and approving each other's feelings, in any event, when we might contradict the substance of their words. By making a safe and non critical space for articulation, we cultivate a climate that energizes weakness, sympathy, and a certifiable craving for goal.

In this chapter, we will explore practical strategies and techniques for effective communication during times of conflict. We will delve into the power of non-violent communication, assertiveness, and active listening as transformative tools to diffuse tension and cultivate understanding. We will also discuss the importance of emotional intelligence in conflict resolution, recognizing and managing our own emotions while remaining attuned to the emotions of our partner.

As you engage with this chapter, take a moment to reflect on your own relationship and the ways in which conflicts have been resolved. Consider the patterns of communication that have emerged and the impact they have had on your connection. Reflect on the areas in which growth and improvement are needed, and the strategies you can employ to foster effective communication during times of conflict. This chapter offers an opportunity for self-reflection and growth, providing insights and practical tools to navigate conflicts with grace and integrity.

Resolving conflict with grace is an ongoing journey, one that requires patience, self-awareness, and a commitment to growth. The following pages will illuminate the transformative power of effective communication, revealing its ability to create a foundation of trust, understanding, and harmony within your relationship.

So, let us embark on this transformative exploration together, with open hearts and open minds, ready to embrace the profound and empowering journey of resolving conflict with grace. May this chapter guide you in developing the communication skills necessary to navigate conflicts with compassion, empathy, and the wisdom to forge a deeper and more resilient bond with your partner.

In any relationship, conflicts and disagreements are inevitable. How couples navigate and resolve these conflicts can significantly impact the health and longevity of their partnership. The topic of "Resolving Conflict with Grace: Strategies for Effective Communication" delves into the importance of constructive conflict resolution and explores strategies that promote healthy communication and resolution of conflicts.

Conflict resolution is an essential aspect of maintaining a harmonious and thriving relationship. Instead of avoiding or suppressing conflicts, couples who approach them with grace and utilize effective communication strategies can transform conflicts into opportunities for growth, understanding, and strengthened bonds.

One key element of resolving conflict with grace is the cultivation of effective communication skills. Partners learn to express their thoughts, emotions, and concerns in a clear, respectful, and non-confrontational manner. They practice active listening, striving to understand each other's perspectives and validate their experiences. Through open and empathetic communication, couples create a safe space where conflicts can be addressed with sincerity and compassion.

Effective communication strategies, such as "I" statements, can play a vital role in conflict resolution. By using "I" statements, partners express their feelings and needs without blaming or attacking the other person. This approach encourages personal responsibility and fosters an atmosphere of understanding and cooperation.

Another crucial aspect of resolving conflicts with grace is the willingness to seek compromise and find win-win solutions. Instead of focusing on "winning" the argument, partners shift their mindset towards finding mutually beneficial resolutions. They engage in collaborative problem-solving, exploring creative options that address the needs and concerns of both individuals. This approach promotes cooperation and fosters a sense of shared responsibility for the relationship's well-being.

Active empathy and understanding are fundamental in conflict resolution. Partners make an effort to step into each other's shoes, seeking to understand the underlying emotions, motivations, and perspectives that contribute to the conflict. They validate each other's feelings, demonstrating genuine care and empathy. By fostering a climate of empathy and understanding, couples create an environment where conflicts can be approached with compassion and a genuine desire to find resolution.

Resolving conflict with grace also involves managing and regulating emotions during disagreements. Partners practice emotional self-regulation, striving to remain calm and composed even in the midst of heated discussions. They take breaks when needed to cool down, gather their thoughts, and approach the conflict with a clear and rational mindset. By managing emotions effectively, couples can prevent conflicts from escalating and damaging the relationship further.

Timing is another crucial factor in conflict resolution. Partners recognize the importance of choosing the right moment to address conflicts, ensuring that both individuals are emotionally available and receptive to the discussion. They create dedicated spaces and times for open and honest communication, free from distractions or external pressures. By considering timing and creating a conducive environment for conflict resolution, couples increase the chances of reaching productive and satisfactory outcomes.

Forgiveness and letting go of grudges play a significant role in resolving conflict with grace. Partners recognize that conflicts are part of the human experience, and holding onto resentments can hinder growth and healing. They practice forgiveness, letting go of past hurts, and moving forward with a renewed commitment to the relationship. By embracing forgiveness, couples create space for healing, understanding, and renewed love.

Resolving conflict with grace is an ongoing process that requires practice, patience, and a genuine desire for growth and harmony.

Couples who adopt these strategies for effective communication and conflict resolution pave the way for a healthier, more resilient, and fulfilling relationship. Through grace, understanding, and a commitment to effective communication, partners can overcome challenges, deepen their connection, and foster a sense of shared growth and happiness.

Conflict is a characteristic piece of any relationship, whether it's with a romantic partner, relative, friend, or colleagues. How we handle conflicts decides the strength and life span of our relationships. In this chapter, we will explore methodologies and procedures to effectively resolve conflicts, advance and understand, and cultivate healthy communication. By creating solid conflict skills, we can explore conflicts and disagreement, fortify our connections, and make an agreeable and satisfying relationship.

1. Figure out the Idea of Conflicts

To really settle conflict in a relationship, it's 6 pivotal to initially grasp the idea of contention itself. Conflicts is a characteristic and unavoidable piece of any relationship, whether it's with a partner, relative, companion, friend and colleagues. Here are central issues to consider while trying to grasp the idea of conflicts:

- **Perceive Conflict As a Chance for Development:**

Conflicts ought to be seen as a chance for development and improvement as opposed to something intrinsically negative. It gives an opportunity to resolve fundamental issues, further develop communication and fortify the relationship. By reexamining conflicts as a likely impetus for positive change, people can move toward it with a more useful mentality.

- **Recognize the Main drivers of Conflicts:**

Conflicts frequently emerge from neglected needs, varying points of view, or irritating issues. It's fundamental to recognize the main drivers of the conflicts instead of zeroing in exclusively on superficial level conflicts. By diving further into the basic elements, people can acquire a more clear understanding of the main things and work towards significant goal.

- **Separate the Individual from the Issue:**

Isolating the individual from the issue during conflicts is significant. Keep away from individual assaults and on second thought center around resolving the particular issues or ways of behaving causing the conflicts. This assists with keeping up with deference and protecting the relationship while tracking down productive arrangements.

- **Embrace Transparent Communication:**

Transparent communication is crucial for seeing each other's viewpoints, requirements, and feelings. Energize open discourse where the two players have a good sense of security offering their viewpoints and sentiments unafraid of judgment or retaliation. Straightforward communication assists with overcoming any barrier and cultivates sympathy and understanding.

- **Practice Dynamic Self Reflection:**

Self reflection is key in figuring out one's own job and commitment to the conflicts. It includes inspecting individual convictions, inclinations, and correspondence styles that might be affecting the conflict. By getting a sense of ownership with one's own decisions and perspectives, people can effectively add to the goal cycle.

- **Look for Intercession if necessary:**

At times, conflict might be mind boggling or well established, making it trying to autonomously track down a goal. Looking for intercession from an unbiased outsider, like an instructor or middle person, can give a protected and organized climate for useful exchange. Arbiters can assist with working with correspondence, recognize shared view, and guide the cycle towards a goal.

- **Split the difference:**

Settling conflict frequently requires split the difference and tracking down center ground. Being available to elective arrangements and ready to make concessions for the relationship is significant. Compromise includes undivided attention, understanding, and tracking down commonly pleasant arrangements that address the necessities and worries of the two players.

By understanding the idea of conflict people can move toward conflict in connection with a more valuable and sympathetic outlook. Perceiving conflict as a chance for development, recognizing underlying drivers, and embracing open openness are absolutely vital for settling conflict effectively. Keep in mind, conflict is a typical piece of human connection, and by moving toward it with understanding and tolerance, people can cultivate more grounded and stronger connections.

2. Develop Successful Communication

Successful communication is the foundation of settling conflict in relationship. It empowers people to offer their viewpoints, feelings, and needs plainly while additionally encouraging understanding and compassion. Here are central issues to consider while developing powerful communication.

- **Practice Undivided Attention:**

Undivided attention is essential for powerful communication. It includes completely captivating in the discussion, focusing on the speaker, and exhibiting understanding. Concentrate completely on the individual talking, keep in touch, and abstain from interfering. Show real interest and interest in their viewpoint. Undivided attention considers a more profound understanding of the other individual's perspective and helps fabricate an establishment for useful discourse.

- **Use "I" Proclamations:**

While communicating your own sentiments and concerns, use "I" articulations rather than "you" explanations. For instance, say, "I feel hurt when this occurs" as opposed to "You generally cause me to feel hurt." "I" proclamations take responsibility for feelings without accusing or blaming the other individual, encouraging a non fierce and valuable discussion.

- **Put Yourself out there Obviously and Deferentially:**

Obviously articulate your thoughts, feelings, and necessities utilizing aware and non fierce language. Be aware of your manner of speaking and nonverbal communication, as they assume a huge part in compelling communication. Try not to utilize forceful or guarded language that might raise the conflict. All things being equal, make progress toward lucidity, graciousness, and assertiveness in putting yourself out there.

- **Approve and Recognize the Other Individual's Point of View:**

Recognize the other individual's point of view by approving and recognizing their perspective. Regardless of whether you dissent, attempt to comprehend what they are used to and recognize the legitimacy of their feelings and encounters. This exhibits compassion and encourages an environment of shared regard.

- **Keep away from Suspicions and Rushing to make Judgment calls:**

Suppositions and rushing to make judgment calls can prompt false impressions and further conflicts. All things being equal, look for explanation by posing unassuming inquiries and effectively trying to grasp the other individual's viewpoint. Challenge your own suppositions and be available to various understandings and conceivable outcomes.

- **Utilize Non Verbal Communication:**

Non verbal signals like looks, non verbal communication, and motions assume a huge part in correspondence. Know about your non verbal signals and guarantee they line up with your expected message. Essentially, focus on the other individual's non verbal prompts to all the more likely grasp their feelings and responses.

- **Practice Sympathetic Tuning in:**

Compassionate listening includes imagining the other individual's perspective and looking to completely figure out their feelings and encounters. Tune in without judgment, and attempt to get a handle on the hidden sentiments and requirements behind their words. Reflect back what you've heard to show that you comprehend and approve their point of view.

- **Enjoy Reprieves When Required:**

Feelings can run high during conflict, making it challenging to successfully impart. Assuming you feel overpowered or notice that the discussion is becoming warmed, have some time off. Move back from the conversation briefly to recover and permit the other individual to do likewise. This break takes into consideration a more useful and quiet discourse when you reconvene.

- **Use Conflict resolution Strategies:**

Find out about conflict resolution methods, for example, dynamic critical thinking, splitting the difference, and looking for shared benefit arrangements. These procedures assist with exploring conflict by tracking down commonly useful results. Practice these strategies to guarantee powerful communication and coordinated effort in settling issues.

By developing viable communication, conflict in relationships can be tended to with lucidity, sympathy, and understanding. Undivided attention, clear articulation, and approval of viewpoints make an establishment for useful exchange. Keep in mind, powerful communication is an expertise that can be created and refined, prompting better and more agreeable connections.

3. Pick the Perfect environment

Picking the perfect environment to address conflicts in relationship is fundamental for viable goal. The climate and timing can fundamentally influence the result of the conversation, so it's critical to make a helpful setting that advances open communication and limits interruptions. Here are central issues to consider while picking the perfect environment:

- **Pick an Impartial and Confidential Setting:**

Select where the two players feel great and safe. Preferably, pick an impartial setting that doesn't incline toward one individual over the other. This could be a calm room at home, a tranquil park, or a confidential space where you can have a continuous discussion. Guaranteeing protection takes into account transparent exchange without the anxiety toward being caught wind of or intruded.

- **Take out Interruptions:**

Limit potential interruptions that could obstruct successful communication. Switch off electronic gadgets or put them on quiet mode to keep away from interferences. Figure out an opportunity when the two people can completely zero in on the conversation without being hurried or engrossed with different obligations. By taking out interruptions, you establish a climate that empowers undivided attention and commitment.

- **Think about Emotional States:**

Be aware of the emotional conditions of the two players while picking the ideal opportunity. It's vital to try not to talk about conflict when either individual is feeling excessively anxious, tired, or overpowered. Feelings can cloud judgment and thwart useful communication. All things being equal, hold back nothing when the two people are somewhat quiet and open to participating in a valuable discussion.

- **Permit Adequate Time:**

Conflict resolution calls for investment and persistence. Pick when there is sufficient accessibility for a top to bottom conversation. Hurrying through the discussion might forestall careful exploration of the issues and block the potential for goal. Designate adequate time for the two players to communicate their points of view, feelings, and concerns completely.

- **Stay away from Public Showdowns:**

Public showdowns can heighten conflict and cause humiliation or distress. It's by and large best to address conflict in private, away from other people. This considers a place of refuge where people can straightforwardly offer their viewpoints and feelings without the feeling of dread toward judgment or exploration from pariahs.

- **Think about Communication Inclinations**:

Consider the communication inclinations of the two players. A few people might favor eye to eye conversations, while others might feel more happy with putting themselves out there through composed communication or innovation-interrupted discussions. Regard each other's communication inclinations and find a strategy that turns out best for the two people.

- **Be Aware of Timing:**

Timing assumes an essential part in conflict resolution. Try not to examine conflict when one or the two players are managing high stress circumstances or during sincerely charged minutes. All things being equal, search for when the two people are moderately quiet and responsive to taking part in a productive exchange.

By picking the perfect set-up for conflicts resolution, you establish a climate that supports open communication, undivided attention, and understanding. An unbiased and confidential setting, liberated from interruptions, considers centered conversations. Being aware of feelings, timing, and communication inclinations adds to a more useful and fruitful goal process. Keep in mind, the right climate makes way for useful discourse and prepares for tracking down commonly pleasant arrangements.

4. Practice and Point of view Taking

Compassion and point of view taking are amazing assets in settling clashes in connections. They permit you to grasp the other individual's feelings, considerations, and encounters, encouraging sympathy and making the way for powerful correspondence and goal.

Here are central issues to consider while rehearsing compassion and viewpoint taking:

- **Come at the situation from Their Perspective:**

Pause for a minute to envision yourself in the other individual's situation. Attempt to grasp their feelings, needs, and concerns. Consider how you would feel on the off chance that you were confronting similar conditions. This exercise develops compassion by permitting you to see what is happening according to their viewpoint.

- **Listen Effectively and Non-Critically:**

While participating in a contention, practice undivided attention. Offer the other individual your unified consideration, keeping in touch and showing veritable interest. Try not to hinder or planning reactions to you while they are talking. All things being equal, center around figuring out their words, feelings, and basic message. Tune in without judgment, permitting them to completely articulate their thoughts.

- **Approve Their Sentiments and Encounters:**

Recognize and approve the other individual's sentiments and encounters, regardless of whether you essentially concur with them. Approve their feelings by saying phrases like, "I can comprehend the reason why you could feel as such" or "Your viewpoint is significant, and I hear you." Approving their sentiments establishes a protected and steady climate for open exchange.

- **Practice Intelligent Reactions:**

Rather than quickly answering the other individual's articulations, practice intelligent reactions. Rework what they have said to show that you really grasp their perspective. Intelligent reactions assist with explaining errors and exhibit your obligation to tuning in and understanding.

- **Develop Interest:**

Move toward the contention with a certified longing to look into the other individual's viewpoint. Pose unconditional inquiries to urge them to share more about their sentiments and encounters. This interest makes a feeling of mental security, cultivating trust and transparency.

- **Separate the Individual from the Issue:**

Recall that the contention is about the main thing, not an individual assault. Separate the individual from the issue to abstain from becoming cautious or participating in private assaults. Perceive that both of you have remarkable viewpoints and legitimate feelings, and the objective is to settle on some mutual interest and resolve the contention together.

- **Think about Social and Individual Contrasts:**

Be aware of social and individual contrasts that might impact the manner in which the other individual sees and answers the contention.

Social foundations, childhood, and individual encounters shape our points of view and ways of behaving. Considering these distinctions develops compassion and advances understanding.

- **Express Compassion and Understanding:**

Whenever you have tuned in and figured out the other individual's point of view, express sympathy and understanding. Use articulations like, "I can perceive how this present circumstance is hard for you" or "I comprehend that this issue means a lot to you." By showing sympathy, you approve their encounters and feelings, reinforcing the establishment for figuring out something worth agreeing on.

- **Look for Split the difference and Shared benefit Arrangements:**

Sympathy and point of view taking set up for finding compromises and shared benefit arrangements. By understanding the other individual's requirements and concerns, you can cooperate towards goals that address the two players' inclinations. Team up and conceptualize thoughts that fulfill every individual's requirements, encouraging a feeling of common regard and understanding.

By rehearsing sympathy and viewpoint taking, clashes in connections can be drawn closer with empathy and understanding. These abilities establish a climate of trust, advance powerful correspondence, and make ready for goal and more grounded associations. Keep in mind, sympathy is an integral asset that overcomes any barrier between contrasting points of view and cultivates agreeable connections.

5. Distinguish the Hidden Issues

During the time spent settling conflict in relationship, it's urgent to distinguish the hidden issues add to the conflict or pressure. By tending to these main drivers, you can actually pursue tracking down dependable arrangements and forestalling future struggles and conflict. Here are central issues to consider while distinguishing the fundamental issues:

- **Look Past Superficial Contentions:**

Conflict frequently emerges from superficial conflicts or episodes, yet there are typically more profound feelings, needs, or values at play. Make a stride back and attempt to recognize the center issues that are powering the conflict. Search for designs or repeating subjects that might reveal insight into the fundamental causes.

- **Practice Self-Reflection:**

Start by looking at your own considerations, feelings, and activities. Ask yourself what might be setting off your reactions or adding to the conflict. Tell the truth and open to self reflection, as this will assist you with acquiring bits of knowledge into your own inspirations and ways of behaving. Understanding yourself better will permit you to move toward the conflict with greater clearness and compassion.

- **Feel for the Other Individual:**

Put yourself in the shoes of the other individual associated with the conflict. Attempt to grasp their point of view, requirements, and feelings. Think about their experience, encounters, and values that might be impacting their activities. Sympathy is an incredible asset for acquiring a more profound understanding of the fundamental issues and cultivating empathy and common regard.

- **Investigate Correspondence Breakdown**

Correspondence breakdowns frequently lie at the core of conflict. Ponder the correspondence designs among you and the other individual. Are there false impressions, misinterpretations, or an absence of powerful correspondence? Search for obstructions that block transparent exchange, like defensiveness, presumptions, or unfortunate listening abilities. Distinguishing these correspondence breakdowns will assist you with tending to them and work on the general nature of correspondence.

- **Reveal Neglected Necessities or Assumptions:**

Clashes and conflict frequently emerge when people have neglected needs or unfulfilled assumptions. Ponder what you or the other individual might be looking for from the relationship or the particular circumstance. Are there implicit longings, stowed away plans, or unexpressed worries? Recognizing these neglected requirements will permit you to address them straightforwardly and pursue finding arrangements that fulfill the two players.

- **Look for Intervention or Expert Assassistance**

Some of the time, recognizing and settling hidden issues might need the support of an impartial outsider, like a go between or specialist. In the event that the conflict appears to be excessively mind boggling or on the other hand assuming that there is a huge power unevenness, looking for proficient assistance can give important bits of knowledge and direction. A prepared middle person or specialist can work with productive conversations and assist with revealing further issues that might be trying to address all alone.

- **Communicate Transparently and Straightforwardly:**

Whenever you have recognized the basic issues, impart them to the next individual in a quiet and non fierce way. Use "I" articulations to communicate your sentiments and concerns, zeroing in on the effect the contention has on you. Urge the other individual to share their viewpoint and feelings also. By encouraging open and straightforward communication, you make a space for understanding and joint effort.

- **Team up on Tracking down Arrangements:**

With a more clear understanding of the fundamental issues, cooperate with the other individual to track down arrangements. Conceptualize thoughts, think about elective methodologies, and be available to think twice about. The objective is to address the main drivers of the conflict and find commonly pleasant goals that fulfill the two players' requirements and encourage a more grounded relationship.

By distinguishing the hidden issues, you can dig further into the center reasons for conflict in relationship. This understanding permits you to move toward the conflict with compassion, open communication and an emphasis on tracking down enduring arrangements. Keep in mind, tending to the main drivers prepares for additional significant and feasible goals, advancing better and more agreeable connections

6. Look for Shared conviction and Split the difference

In settling clashes and conflict in relationship looking for shared conviction and finding compromises are urgent strides towards tracking down commonly pleasing arrangements. It requires an eagerness to comprehend and regard the viewpoints and necessities of the two players included. Here are central issues to consider while looking for shared conviction and taking part in split the difference:

- **Distinguish Shared Interests:**

Start by recognizing shared interests or objectives that the two players can energize behind. Search for normal qualities, wants, or goals that can act as an establishment for tracking down center ground. At the point when you center around shared interests, it becomes more straightforward to move the discussion towards finding arrangements that fulfill the two players.

- **Practice Undivided attention:**

Take part in undivided attention to comprehend the other individual's perspective and concerns really. Offer them your unified consideration, keep in touch, and show sympathy. By effectively tuning in, you establish a climate of regard and receptiveness that empowers productive discourse and exchange.

- **Embrace Adaptability:**

Adaptability is fundamental in tracking down splits the difference. It requires being available to various thoughts and taking into account elective viewpoints. Relinquish unbending positions and investigate savvy fixes that can address the necessities of the two players. Embracing adaptability advances a helpful environment where goal turns out to be more feasible.

- **Work together for Shared benefit Arrangements:**

Hold back nothing arrangements where the two players feel their requirements are met. Rather than moving toward the contention as a success lose situation, encourage an outlook of joint effort. Empower conceptualizing and critical thinking together, permitting space for inventive thoughts and approaches. By cooperating, you can show up at arrangements that go past simple split the difference and make positive results for all interested parties.

- **Impart Confidently:**

Powerful communication is urgent while looking for a shared view and splitting the difference. Obviously express your requirements, concerns, and thoughts, while additionally being available to hearing the other individual's point of view. Use "I" proclamations to convey your sentiments and keep away from accusatory language that can raise pressures. Take a stab at a deferential and decisive correspondence style that encourages understanding and collaboration.

- **Focus on the Relationship:**

Recall that the actual relationship is significant and ought to be vital. Some of the time, the significance of keeping a solid and agreeable association offsets individual longings or inclinations. Consider the drawn out ramifications of the contention and the effect it might have on the relationship. This point of view can assist with directing you towards arrangements that safeguard the bond and encourage shared development.

- **Figure out the Craft of Give and take:**

Compromise includes finding a center ground where the two players settle on concessions to agree. It requires an eagerness to surrender specific longings or inclinations for settling the contention and conflict. Look for regions where you can compromise, tracking down arrangements that balance the requirements and needs of the two players. Recall that compromise isn't tied in with forfeiting everything except about tracking down a fair and sensible goal.

- **Assess and Change:**

Subsequent to arriving at a split the difference, assess its viability over the long run. Evaluate whether the settled upon arrangement is working for the two players and be available to change if vital. Relationships advance, and clashes might require progressing assessment and variation. Keep up with open lines of communication to address any worries or issues that might emerge, guaranteeing that the trade off stays supportable and acceptable.

By looking for a shared view and participating in split the difference, clashes and conflict in relationships can be settled in a way that regards the necessities and viewpoints of the two players. It requires undivided attention, adaptability, joint effort, and a guarantee to finding shared benefit arrangements. Keep in mind, the objective isn't to "win" the contention yet to find goals that fortify the relationship and advance amicability, harmony, growth and development.

7. Practice Forgiveness and Giving up

Forgiveness and giving up are crucial parts of conflict resolution and fundamental for keeping up with a solid relationship. Clutching disdain and complaints can propagate conflict and upset the way to goal. Here are a few central issues to consider while rehearsing pardoning and giving up:

- **Comprehending the Power of Forgiveness:**

Forgiveness is a cognizant decision to deliver gloomy sentiments and hatred towards the other individual. It doesn't mean supporting or pardoning their way of behaving yet rather liberating yourself from the close to home weight that the conflict conveys. Perceive that forgiveness is a gift you provide for yourself, permitting you to push ahead and recuperate.

- **Ponder Your Feelings:**

Carve out opportunity to think about your feelings and the effect the contention and conflict has had on you. Grasp that clutching outrage, hurt, or hatred just drags out the adverse consequences of the conflict. Recognize your feelings and permit yourself to feel them, yet additionally perceive the significance of delivering them for your own prosperity.

- **Practice Self-Empathy:**

Indulge yourself with thoughtfulness and sympathy during the course of forgiveness. Comprehend that no one's perfect and that clutching feelings of spite just damages you over the long haul. Embrace self forgiveness , recognizing that you, as well, are equipped for development and gaining from clashes.

- **Impart and Communicate Sentiments:**

If suitable, speak with the other individual about your sentiments and the effect of the conflict. Put yourself out there genuinely and self-assuredly, underlining your longing for goal and pushing ahead. This communication can assist with making understanding and prepare for forgiveness.

- **Let Go of the Requirement for Control:**

Frequently, clashes emerge from a craving for control or they should be legitimized. Relinquish the need to control what is happening or the other individual's activities. Comprehend that you can't change the past, yet you have command over your reaction and your future activities. Center around how you might advance the circumstance as opposed to harping on past complaints.

- **Practice Appreciation and Inspiration:**

Develop appreciation for the positive parts of the relationship and the examples gained from the contention. Shift your concentration towards the qualities and positive characteristics of the other individual. Embrace energy and hopefulness, permitting yourself to push ahead with a new point of view.

- **Look for Conclusion:**

Now and again, looking for a conclusion can be useful in forgiveness process. This might include having a discussion with the other individual to communicate your forgiveness and commitment to push ahead. Notwithstanding, conclusion can likewise be accomplished inside by pursuing a cognizant choice to give up and deliver the pessimistic feelings attached to the conflict.

- **Gain from the Conflict:**

Each conflict gives an open door to self-improvement and learning. Think about the conflict and recognize any examples or bits of knowledge acquired from the experience. Utilize this newly discovered information to further develop your relational abilities, put down stopping points, or address any basic issues that added to the contention.

Practicing forgiveness and giving up calls for investment, exertion, and self-reflection. An interaction permits you to deliver cynicism, advance mending, and make space for a better and more amicable relationship. By embracing pardoning, you enable yourself to push ahead with sympathy and figuring out, cultivating a more certain and versatile association with others.

8. Use Conflict Resolution Procedures

Conflict resolution procedures give organized ways to deal with address and resolve conflicts. These methods assist with directing discussions and encourage useful communication. Here are some compelling conflicts resolution methods to consider:

- **Mutual benefit Approach:**

In conflict, it's vital to move from a success-lose mindset to a mutually beneficial mindset. Rather than zeroing in on one individual's triumph over the other, go for the gold that benefits the two players. Team up to track down innovative other options and compromises that address the issues and interests of all interested parties. This approach advances participation, constructs trust, and reinforces the relationship.

- **Dynamic Critical thinking:**

Separate the conflict into explicit issues that can be tended to and settled. Empower open exchange where the two players can offer their points of view and concerns. Explore potential arrangements together and conceptualize thoughts. Center around finding functional and practical arrangements that fulfill the interests of the two people. Effectively take part in critical thinking as opposed to becoming involved with fault or protectiveness.

- **Split the difference:**

Once in a while conflict requires tracking down center ground and arriving at a split the difference. Each party might have to make concessions and provide up something to arrive at a commonly satisfactory arrangement. This includes effectively paying attention to one another's points of view, figuring out the basic requirements, and tracking down an equilibrium that regards the interests of the two people. Conflict resolution requires adaptability and an eagerness to track down an answer that fulfills the two players somewhat.

- **Intervention**:

In circumstances where direct communication between the clashing gatherings becomes troublesome or incapable, consider including an unbiased outsider as a middle person. An arbiter can work with the discussion, guarantee that every individual has a chance to talk and be heard, and guide the interaction toward a goal. Arbiters give an objective viewpoint and can assist with exploring the feelings and strains associated with the conflict. They help with settling on some shared interest and arriving at a commonly pleasing result.

- **Intercession:**

In circumstances where direct communication between the clashing gatherings becomes troublesome or incapable, consider including an impartial outsider as a middle person. A go between can work with the discussion, guarantee that every individual has a chance to talk and be heard, and guide the interaction toward a goal. Arbiters give an objective point of view and can assist with exploring the feelings and strains associated with the contention. They help with figuring out some shared interest and arriving at a commonly pleasant result.

- **Undivided attention and Intelligent Reactions:**

Successful communication is at the center of conflict resolution. Practice undivided attention by concentrating on the other individual and really figuring out their viewpoint. Utilize intelligent reactions to show that you have grasped their perspective and feelings. Intelligent reactions can incorporate summing up their viewpoints, posing, explaining inquiries, and communicating compassion. This approach advances understanding and approves the other individual's encounters, encouraging a more useful and deferential discourse.

- **Look for Proficient Assistance:**

In complex or profoundly settled in clashes, looking for proficient assistance from a specialist, guide, or middle person can be valuable. These experts have specific preparation in compromise and can give direction and backing. They can assist you with exploring testing elements, reveal fundamental issues, and work with viable correspondence techniques. Looking for proficient assistance shows a guarantee to tracking down a goal and working on the relationship.

Remember, conflict resolution is an ongoing process that requires patience, empathy, and a genuine desire to understand and collaborate. It's important to be open to different perspectives and be willing to find common ground. By applying these conflict resolution techniques, you can transform conflicts into opportunities for growth, strengthen relationships, and create a more harmonious and fulfilling connection with others.

Resolving conflicts in relationships is not always easy, but it is essential for the health and longevity of our connections. By implementing effective communication strategies, practicing empathy, seeking common ground, and utilizing conflict resolution techniques, we can navigate conflicts with grace and integrity.

Throughout this chapter, we have explored the importance of understanding the nature of conflict, cultivating open communication, choosing the right time and place for discussions, and practicing empathy and perspective-taking. We have also discussed the significance of identifying underlying issues, seeking common ground, and using techniques such as compromise and mediation.

Additionally, we highlighted the importance of practicing forgiveness and letting go. The power of forgiveness lies in its ability to release negative emotions and free ourselves from the weight of unresolved conflicts. By embracing forgiveness, we create the opportunity for healing, growth, and the strengthening of our relationships.

Conflict resolution is not about avoiding conflicts altogether, but rather about navigating them with respect, understanding, and a commitment to finding resolution. It requires active listening, effective communication, and a willingness to collaborate. When conflicts arise, we must remember that they can be opportunities for growth, deeper understanding, and strengthened connections.

As we conclude this chapter, let us remember that resolving conflicts in relationships is an ongoing process. It requires patience, self-reflection, and a dedication to maintaining open lines of communication. By applying the principles and techniques discussed, we can cultivate healthier and more fulfilling relationships, where conflicts are approached as opportunities for growth rather than as obstacles.

In the end, conflict resolution is not just about finding a quick fix or a temporary solution. It is about nurturing understanding, fostering empathy, and creating an environment of respect and collaboration. By embracing these principles and actively practicing conflict resolution, we can cultivate stronger, more resilient relationships that stand the test of time.

Remember, conflicts are inevitable in relationships, but how we approach and resolve them defines the strength and depth of our connections. With the tools and strategies provided in this chapter, you are equipped to navigate conflicts with confidence, compassion, and the commitment to finding resolution. Embrace the journey of conflict resolution and watch as your relationships thrive and flourish.

Chapter 5

Overcoming Challenges Together: Support and Teamwork

In the diverse weaving of a reliable and long lasting relationship, challenges undeniably arise, testing the strength of our obligation and the significance of our relationship. It is during these minutes that the power of help and participation becomes crucial. In this part, "Overcoming Challenges Together: Support and Teamwork," we leave on a historic examination of how we can explore the difficulties of life as a bound together front, finding strength, adaptability, and improvement despite setbacks.

Challenges are the intersection where we end up at a slope - they can either crack our bond or become venturing stones towards a more grounded, really persevering through relationship. It is through the force of help and collaboration that we can change these difficulties into open doors for development and shared wins. This section and chapter dives profound into the meaning of developing a partnership established on faithful help, trust, and a common feeling of direction, perceiving that it is even with difficulties that we find the genuine strength of our connection

Support is the soul of a relationship, the unshakable groundwork whereupon we incline in the midst of vulnerability and uncertainty. The steady presence of a partner who supports us during the tempest, offering a listening ear, a soothing hug, and an unfaltering faith in our capacities. Support implies being each other's greatest team promoters, praising triumphs and offering comfort during routes. It is a demonstration of adoration and responsibility, establishing a climate of wellbeing and security where development and mending can prosper.

Yet, support alone isn't sufficient. The union of help and cooperation drives us forward as a unified power. Cooperation is the cooperative work to explore difficulties, pooling together our assets, abilities, and resources. It is the acknowledgment that when we join our singular limits, we make a power more noteworthy than the amount of its parts. Through cooperation, we tap into the aggregate insight and critical thinking capacities conflicted working as one. It requires compelling communication, common regard, and a common readiness to defy difficulties head-on.

In this part, we will research utilitarian systems and pieces of information for empowering help and joint effort inside your relationship. We will plunge into the meaning of effective communication making a safe space for shortcoming and responsiveness. We will similarly discuss the significance of full focus, compassion, and endorsement as crucial gadgets for offering the assistance and backing that our accessories need during testing times. Besides, we will explore the power of shared goals and a total vision, seeing that an internal compass can secure us during the stormiest of times.

As you attract this part, stop briefly to consider your own relationship and the way you have maintained each other through challenges. Consider the locales where further turn of events and improvement are required, and the systems you can use to energize solid areas for help and participation. This segment invites self-reflection and personal growth, offering pieces of information and sensible instruments to overcome hardships as a brought together front.

Vanquishing troubles together is a nonstop journey, one that requires liability, strength, and a typical vision. The going with pages will edify the remarkable power of help and participation, revealing their ability to fabricate commitments of undaunted strength and develop advancement and flexibility inside your relationship.

Hence, let us set out on this phenomenal examination together, with open hearts and responsive standpoints, ready to embrace the critical and empowering journey of overcoming troubles together. May this part guide you in fostering an association in view of unfazed help, trust, and a typical internal compass, engaging you to vanquish any hindrance that comes your way.

The in-depth investigation aims to provide a deeper comprehension of how couples can strengthen their bonds, cultivate resilience, and provide support for one another during trying times. It emphasizes the significance of collaborative effort, empathy, and efficient communication in overcoming challenges and enhancing a marriage's foundation.

Compelling correspondence is essential for couples to communicate their sentiments, concerns, and needs. It allows partners to connect on a deeper level and discover common ground because it involves active listening, genuine understanding, and open dialogue. By participating in significant discussions, couples can explore difficulties with clearness, sympathy, and a common vision for goal.

Sympathy assumes an imperative part in offering profound help and grasping in a marriage and relationship. Recognizing and validating one's partner's experiences, emotions, and perspectives necessitates the ability to put oneself in their shoes. Couples can create a safe and supportive environment where they can feel heard, seen, and valued even in the face of adversity by developing empathy.

Cooperation is the foundation of collaboration in marriage and relationships. It entails collaborating, utilizing one another's strengths, and coming up with collective solutions to the issues at hand. Couples can overcome challenges with a sense of shared purpose and resilience by utilizing each other's unique abilities and strengths.

The study emphasizes that conflict resolution and quick fixes are not the only ways to overcome challenges in marriage. Commitment, perseverance, and a willingness to grow together are all necessary for this transformative process. Couples have a chance to build a relationship that can withstand the test of time and deepen their bond by accepting the journey of overcoming obstacles.

In the end, the goal of the study is to motivate couples to confront obstacles head-on and view them as opportunities for growth and strengthening their marriage and relationship. It gives couples insight, useful tools, and motivation to grow support and teamwork, allowing them to overcome challenges with grace, compassion, and unity. Through this excursion, couples can cultivate a marriage that flourishes despite difficulties, making a strong starting point for an enduring and satisfying relationship.

Effective communication is crucial for couples to express their feelings, concerns, and needs. It involves active listening, genuine understanding, and open dialogue, allowing partners to connect on a deeper level and find common ground. By engaging in meaningful conversations, couples can navigate challenges with clarity, empathy, and a shared vision for resolution.

Empathy plays a vital role in providing emotional support and understanding in a marriage. It involves the ability to step into each other's shoes, recognizing and validating the experiences, emotions, and perspectives of one's partner. By cultivating empathy, couples can create a safe and supportive space where they feel heard, seen, and valued, even in the face of adversity.

Collaboration is the cornerstone of teamwork in marriage and relationships. It entails working together, pooling strengths, and finding collective solutions to the challenges at hand. By leveraging each other's unique abilities and strengths, couples can approach obstacles with a shared sense of purpose, fostering a sense of unity and resilience.

The exploration emphasizes overcoming challenges in marriage and is not about avoiding conflict or seeking quick fixes. It is a transformative process that requires commitment, patience, and a willingness to grow together. By embracing the journey of overcoming challenges, couples have an opportunity to deepen their bond, strengthen their connection, and forge a relationship that can withstand the tests of time.

Cooperation and teamwork, then again, is the cooperative work to handle difficulties as a brought together power. It is the acknowledgment that we are more grounded together than we are separated. Through collaboration and teamwork, partners influence their singular assets and abilities to track down arrangements, share the heap, and explore snags with a feeling of solidarity and common perspective. It requires open communication, an eagerness to think twice about, a profound feeling of confidence in one another's capacities and goals

Relationship is a consecrated association that unites two people, restricting them in a guarantee to explore life's process as partners. A wonderful and extraordinary responsibility holds inside it the potential for massive development, happiness, and love. Nonetheless, this way isn't generally smooth, and each couple will confront difficulties along the way

Marriage and relationship isn't an objective; it is a common experience loaded up with pinnacles and valleys, wins and difficulties. It is at these times of trouble that the genuine strength of a partnership is uncovered. When confronted with difficulties, couples have the chance to draw upon their aggregate strength, profound love, and steady obligation to help and elevate each other.

Defeating difficulties together isn't just about tracking down arrangements or staying away from struggle. It is tied in with embracing a mentality of collaboration, where the partners are focused on supporting and elevating each other through various challenges. It is an encouragement to develop a profound feeling of sympathy, understanding, and empathy, as we face the obstructions that life tosses our direction.

Defeating difficulties together isn't just about tracking down arrangements or staying away from struggle. It is tied in with embracing a mentality of collaboration, where the two partners are focused on supporting and elevating each other through various challenges.

It is an encouragement to develop a profound feeling of sympathy, understanding, and empathy, as we face the obstructions that life tosses our direction.

Besides, we adventure into the domain of cooperation, understanding that a solid relationship requires dynamic support and shared liabilities. We investigate the craft of critical thinking together, looking for innovative and commonly helpful arrangements that honor the two people's necessities and wants. We figure out how to commend each other's assets and explore shortcomings, perceiving that together, we can overcome any deterrent that comes our direction.

Ultimately, the exploration seeks to inspire couples to face challenges head-on, viewing them as opportunities for growth and strengthening their marital bond. It offers insights, practical tools, and inspiration to cultivate support and teamwork, enabling couples to navigate obstacles with grace, compassion, and unity. Through this journey, couples can foster a marriage that thrives in the face of challenges, creating a solid foundation for a lasting and fulfilling partnership.

Chapter 6

Forgiving and Healing: The Path to Renewed Love

In the weaving of a sturdy and long lasting relationship, there will without a doubt be depictions of hurt, disappointment, and even traitorousness. These horrifying experiences can shake the genuine support of our reverence, leaving us questioning whether recovering and re-energizing are possible. In this part, "Forgiving and Healing: The Path to Renewed Love," we forget about an exceptional trip of figuring, compassion, and advancement, exploring the critical power of exonerating in restoring and resuscitating our affiliation.

Healing is a delicate yet weighty exhibition, one that can fix the wrecked pieces of our spirits and reignite the fire of love. It is a discerning choice to convey scorn, shock, and the hankering for retaliation, allowing recovering to happen inside ourselves and inside our relationship. Exculpating is unquestionably not a straightforward method for strolling, but it is a crucial one expecting we wish to push ahead and recuperate the pleasure and closeness that once flourished.

Exactly when we excuse, we perceive that our accessory, like ourselves, is human and slight. We see that mistakes and staggers are a piece of the human experience, and clutching scorn simply engenders the disturbance. Forgiveness is a show of compassion, loosening up understanding and empathy to our accessory's defects and deficiencies. It is a vow to surrender the past and account for improvement, patching, and re-energized love.

Healing is a crucial piece of the exculpating adventure. It incorporates perceiving our exacerbation, allowing ourselves to regret, and actually seeking after redoing trust and restoring near and dear flourishing. Forgiveness is a cycle that requires resistance, dealing with oneself, and open communication. It requires making a safe space where the two partners can impart their sentiments, share their shortcomings, and work together to redo the supporting of trust and closeness.

In this part, we will examine the noteworthy power of forgiving and healing inside a relationship. We will plunge into the up close and personal and mental pieces of exculpating, understanding the impediments that disappoint our ability to forgive and the means we can take to overcome them. We will in like manner explore the occupation of compassion, sympathy, and open communication in the exculpating framework, seeing that veritable recovery requires a genuine understanding of our accessory's perspective and a working commitment to change the wrecked pieces.

Also, we will discuss the meaning of self-exonerating, seeing that healing can't be done without loosening up compassion and exculpation to ourselves. We will research the practices and systems that advance self-reflection, self-compassion, and personal development, allowing us to convey culpability and shame and embrace a reestablished character worth.

As you attract this part, stop briefly to consider your own relationship and the districts where forgiving and healing may be required. Think about the exacerbation and wounds that pause, and the means you can take to leave on the method of pardon. This segment invites you to embrace the earth shattering power of exculpation and retouching, to convey the weight of past harms, and to not keep anything away from the opportunity of re-energized love.

Forgiving and Healing is a fearless and liberating adventure, one that requires shortcoming, strength, and a significant commitment to the improvement of your relationship. The going with pages will edify the earth shattering power of acquitting, revealing its ability to restore trust, develop compassion, and plan for a love that is more grounded and more grounded than at some other time.

Hence, let us leave on this historic examination together, with open hearts and responsive viewpoints, ready to embrace the huge and empowering journey of forgiveness and healing. May this part guide you in fostering a relationship that twists with compassion, understanding, and the boundless potential for restoration and improvement.

Forgiving and Healing: The Path of Renewed Love in Relationship" investigates the extraordinary force of forgiveness and healing in fixing and renewing relationships that have encountered harm, double-crossing, or agony. It digs into the most common way of giving up, healing profound injuries, and rediscovering affection and connection.

The broad exploration means to reveal insight into the significance of forgiveness as an impetus for healing and recharging love in connections. It recognizes that struggles and harmful encounters are unavoidable seeing someone yet stresses that pardoning offers a way towards goal, development, and the reclamation of adoration and trust.

Forgiveness is a cognizant decision to deliver disdain, outrage, and harshness towards one's partner. It includes embracing sympathy, empathy, and an eagerness to relinquish past damages. By excusing, people free themselves up to recuperating and making space for reestablished love to thrive.

Healing is a fundamental part of the pardoning system. It includes tending to close to home injuries, revamping trust, and supporting the prosperity of the two people in the relationship. Recuperating requires thoughtfulness, self-reflection, and a pledge to self-improvement. It frequently includes looking for proficient assistance, participating in treatment, or using self improvement assets to explore the complicated feelings that emerge from past damages.

The exploration features that generous and recuperating is a common excursion in a relationship. The two partners assume a functioning part simultaneously, recognizing their own slip-ups, assuming liability, and stretching out pardoning to each other. It requires transparent communication weakness, and a certifiable craving to modify and reestablish the adoration that at first united the couple.

Recharged love rises up out of the profundities of forgiveness and mending. An affection has been tried and changed, an affection that can possibly be significantly more grounded and stronger than previously. Through the course of forgiveness and healing, couples can revive their connection, develop how they might interpret one another, and develop a relationship based on trust, sympathy, and restored love.

The exploration looks to give bits of knowledge, direction, and motivation to people who have encountered relationship challenges and are looking for a way towards forgiveness and healing. It underscores that forgiveness is certainly not a simple or momentary interaction yet a groundbreaking excursion that requires persistence, compassion, and a promise to individual and social development.

By setting out on the way of excusing and healing, couples can track down comfort, discharge profound weights, and rediscover the excellence of adoration. It is a valuable chance to make a future together in view of sympathy, understanding, and the versatility that comes from exploring difficulties and arising more grounded as a unified couple.

Eventually, "Forgiveness and Healing: The path to Renewed Love", urges couples to embrace forgiveness, leave on the excursion of healing, and hold nothing back from the chance of a recharged and extended love that rises above past damages. It is an exploration of trust, rebuilding, and the extraordinary power if forgiveness chasing after enduring and satisfying connections.

Relationships are intricate and dynamic, and it is not uncommon for conflicts, betrayals, or hurtful experiences to occur. When trust is broken, wounds are inflicted, and emotions are raw, the path to renewed love may seem uncertain or even unreachable. However, forgiveness and healing offer a powerful pathway towards restoring love, trust, and emotional well-being.

Forgiveness is a deeply personal and courageous choice. It involves letting go of resentment, anger, and the desire for revenge, and instead, embracing empathy, compassion, and understanding. It is not about condoning the hurtful actions or forgetting the pain but rather choosing to release the emotional burden that comes with holding onto past grievances. Through forgiveness, individuals can free themselves from the weight of negativity and open up space for healing and renewal.

Healing is an essential component of the forgiveness process. It involves tending to emotional wounds, addressing unresolved issues, and working towards restoring the emotional well-being of both individuals in the relationship. Healing requires self-reflection, introspection, and a commitment to personal growth. It may involve seeking professional help, engaging in therapy, or utilizing self-help resources to navigate complex emotions, rebuild trust, and develop healthier patterns of relating.

The journey of forgiveness and healing is not linear or without its challenges. It requires time, patience, and a willingness to confront painful emotions and face difficult conversations. It may involve acknowledging one's own role in the relationship dynamics and taking responsibility for personal actions. It also requires a genuine desire to restore and rebuild the foundation of love and trust.

Renewed love emerges from the depths of forgiveness and healing. It is a love that has been tested, transformed, and rekindled. It is a love that is more resilient, compassionate, and mature. Through the process of forgiveness and healing, couples can deepen their understanding of one another, develop greater empathy and vulnerability, and cultivate a relationship that is rooted in authenticity, growth, and renewed love.

The exploration of "Forgiving and Healing: The Path to Renewed Love in Relationships" offers insights, strategies, and inspiration for individuals who seek to embark on this transformative journey. It emphasizes that forgiveness is a choice and a process that requires courage, self-reflection, and a commitment to personal and relational growth. It encourages open and honest communication, active listening, and a willingness to understand and validate each other's experiences and emotions.

By embracing the path of forgiving and healing, couples can create a future together that is grounded in trust, compassion, and renewed love. They can develop a stronger bond, establish healthier relationship patterns, and find solace in the shared journey of growth and renewal. Ultimately, forgiveness and healing pave the way for a relationship that is built on a solid foundation of understanding, acceptance, and the profound power of love.

Part III

Cultivating a Flourishing Partnership

Chapter 7

Growing Together: The Art of Continuous Relationship Growth

A trustworthy relationship is certainly not a flat component yet a straightforward bond that endlessly creates after some time. Comparatively as individuals create and change, so too do the components inside a serious partnership In this part, "Growing Together: The Art of Continuous Relationship Growth," we set out on an earth shattering examination of the wonderfulness and need of embracing improvement collectively, supporting a relationship that twists through the hours of life.

Relationship improvement is a constant journey, a dance between two individuals zeroed in on supporting each other's mindfulness and the progression of their normal affiliation. It is a delicate balance of regarding the particular ways while developing a significant sensation of concordance and shared desires. The specialty of steady relationship improvement lies in embracing change, lauding accomplishments, and making a space where the two associates can succeed as individuals and as a couple.

As we leave on this phenomenal outing, it is basic to see that advancement is troubled or straightforward always. It requires self-reflection, shortcoming, and an energy to embrace new experiences and perspectives. Improvement moves us to face our sensations of anxiety, break freed from limiting convictions, and develop our capacity for veneration, compassion, and understanding. It is through this course of improvement that we can make a relationship that isn't simply extreme yet likewise significantly fulfilling and huge.

In this part, we will explore the various parts of relationship improvement and growth and the specialty of supporting endless advancement collectively. We will plunge into the meaning of open communication where genuine trade transforms into a vehicle for imparting desires, needs, and individual necessities. We will in like manner look at the importance of shared targets and values, seeing that an ability to know east from west and ordinary vision can go about as a coordinating light all through the journey of improvement.

Besides, we will research the occupation of mindfulness inside the setting of a relationship. We will view the meaning of care, dealing with oneself, and self-awareness as essential pieces of individual turn of events, seeing that when the two accessories are centered around their own outings, the relationship in everyday benefits. We will moreover look at the possibility of dependence, understanding that while individual improvement is basic, it is in the joining of lives, dreams, and desires that a truly vigorous and creating organization is formed.

As you attract this part, stop briefly to consider your own relationship and the areas where advancement and improvement can be upheld. Consider your particular objectives and how they line up with the normal vision you hold collectively. Consider the way you can maintain and uphold each other's personal growth, empowering an environment of constant learning, examination, and change.

Turning out to be together is a support to embrace the continuously changing nature of life and love. It is a confirmation that improvement is certainly not a goal anyway a dependable journey, one that solicitations interest, adaptability, and a significant commitment to each other's success and fulfillment. The going with pages will edify the momentous power of tireless relationship advancement, uncovering its ability to support the bond, energize individual flourishing, and make a reverence that reaches out over the long haul.

Subsequently, let us set out on this notable examination together, with open hearts and responsive standpoints, ready to embrace the critical and empowering journey of turning out to be together. May this part guide you in supporting a relationship that twists with the eminence of steady turn of events, where love and sponsorship weave to make an affiliation that perseveres over the super long stretch and blossoms in each season of life.

The topic of "Growing Together: The Art of Continuous Relationship Growth" explores the dynamic process of nurturing and cultivating a relationship that evolves and flourishes over time. It delves into the essential elements, attitudes, and practices that contribute to the ongoing growth and development of a partnership.

At the heart of continuous relationship growth is the recognition that relationships are not static entities but living organisms that require care, attention, and investment. It starts with a shared commitment from both partners to prioritize the growth and well-being of the relationship. This commitment lays the foundation for a thriving and fulfilling partnership.

In the journey of a long-lasting relationship, growth is not a destination but rather a continuous process. It is an active and intentional effort to deepen the connection, strengthen the bond, and foster personal and relational growth. The exploration of this topic aims to provide insights, strategies, and inspiration for individuals seeking to embark on the path of continuous relationship growth.

Continuous relationship growth begins with a commitment to individual growth. Each partner acknowledges the importance of personal development, self-awareness, and self-improvement. By prioritizing self-growth, individuals bring their best selves into the relationship, contributing to the overall health and vitality of the partnership.

One of the key elements in the art of continuous relationship growth is effective and open communication. Partners engage in honest and authentic conversations, expressing their thoughts, feelings, and needs with vulnerability and empathy. They actively listen to each other, seek to understand and validate their experiences, and engage in constructive dialogue. Communication serves as a vehicle for connection, understanding, and resolution, allowing the relationship to evolve and adapt to new circumstances.

Another essential aspect of continuous growth is the cultivation of shared values and goals.

Partners collaboratively identify their core values, principles, and aspirations, and work towards aligning their individual paths to create a common vision for their relationship. By fostering shared goals, couples establish a sense of purpose and direction, which fuels their growth and provides a sense of unity and cohesion.

Communication is a fundamental aspect of growing together. Open and honest communication allows partners to express their needs, desires, and concerns, fostering a sense of understanding and connection. Effective communication involves active listening, empathy, and the ability to navigate differences and conflicts constructively. It is a tool for deepening intimacy and maintaining a strong emotional connection.

Cultivating shared values and goals is another vital component of relationship growth. Partners work collaboratively to identify and pursue common aspirations, whether they are related to career, family, personal growth, or shared experiences. By aligning their visions, couples create a sense of purpose and direction that nurtures their growth as a unit.

Embracing change and adaptability is essential in the art of continuous relationship growth. Relationships evolve over time, and partners need to be flexible, willing to adjust, and adapt to new circumstances and challenges. This includes navigating life transitions, embracing new roles and responsibilities, and supporting each other through the ups and downs that come with growth and change.

A growth mindset is crucial for continuous relationship growth. It involves a willingness to learn, unlearn, and relearn as individuals and as a couple. A growth mindset fosters curiosity, open-mindedness, and a sense of possibility, allowing partners to explore new experiences, expand their perspectives, and evolve together.

Nurturing emotional intimacy is a cornerstone of relationship growth. It involves creating a safe space for vulnerability, trust, and deep connection. Emotional intimacy is cultivated through acts of kindness, appreciation, and attentiveness to each other's emotional needs. It is a foundation for building a strong bond and fostering ongoing growth and closeness.

Self-reflection and self-awareness play a vital role in continuous relationship growth. Individuals take time to reflect on their thoughts, emotions, and patterns of behavior, seeking to understand themselves better and how they contribute to the relationship dynamics. Self-awareness allows partners to take responsibility for their actions, communicate their needs effectively, and make intentional choices that contribute to the growth of the relationship.

Growing together is not without its challenges. It requires patience, commitment, and a willingness to embrace discomfort and uncertainty. Partners need to be supportive of each other's individual journeys, providing encouragement, and celebrating each other's growth and achievements.

Challenges and setbacks are inevitable in any relationship, and overcoming them is an integral part of continuous growth. Partners approach obstacles as opportunities for learning and development. They navigate conflicts with respect, empathy, and a commitment to finding mutually beneficial solutions. They seek support from each other, utilize resources such as counseling or therapy when needed, and persevere through difficulties, knowing that growth often emerges from moments of challenge.

The exploration of "Growing Together: The Art of Continuous Relationship Growth" serves as a guide for individuals who aspire to create a relationship that thrives and evolves over time. It offers insights, practical tools, and inspiration to foster personal growth, strengthen the connection, and nurture a partnership that is resilient, fulfilling, and continuously growing.

Ultimately, continuous relationship growth is a lifelong commitment to mutual support, understanding, and shared exploration. It is an art that requires dedication, intentionality, and a deep appreciation for the ever-changing nature of love and partnership. By embracing the art of growing together, couples can create a relationship that enriches their lives, brings joy and fulfillment, and stands the test of time.

Chapter 8

Keeping the Romance Alive: Reigniting Passion and Love.

In the journey of a dependable relationship, there might come when the flares of energy and sentiment flash, eclipsed by the requests and schedules of day to day existence. The underlying energy and force might disappear, leaving us longing to reignite the flash that once lighted our affection. In this section, "Keeping the Romance Alive: Reigniting Passion and Love," we set out on an extraordinary exploration of how to revive our relationship, supporting a connection that keeps on flourishing with energy, closeness, and sincerity.

Romance is the specialty of keeping the heart ablaze, of mixing ordinary minutes with the magic love. It is the doorway to more intimacy and connection, making a feeling of bliss, fervor, and yearning inside the relationship. Keeping the romance alive requires expectation, exertion, and a veritable longing to focus on the emotional and actual connection that lies at the center of our love.

Reigniting passion and love isn't tied in with reproducing the past, however about embracing the present with a recharged feeling of miracle and appreciation. It includes finding better approaches to communicate love, developing customs and customs that sustain the connection, and making a space where the two partners can completely explore and enjoy the profundities of their longings and dreams.

In this part, we will leave on a broad exploration of the components that add to keeping the romance alive inside a relationship. We will dig into the significance of sustaining emotional in where genuine communication, weakness, and profound figuring out establish the groundwork for an enthusiastic connection. We will likewise examine the meaning of actual friendship, contact, and closeness as fundamental fixings in touching off the flashes of want and reigniting the fire of enthusiasm.

Moreover, we will explore the specialty of shock and immediacy, perceiving that infusing curiosity and fervor into the relationship can revive the feeling of experience and keep the flares of enthusiasm shining brilliantly. We will dive into the force of shared encounters, making important minutes together that fortify the bond and make enduring associations.

As you draw in with this part, pause for a minute to ponder your own relationship and the regions where the romance can be reignited. Think about the little motions, the genuine articulations of adoration, and the common encounters that can restore the flash and develop the connection. Think about the manners by which you can focus on romance, make space for enthusiasm, and develop a climate that praises the magnificence and sorcery of affection.

Keeping the sentiment alive is an encouragement to inject your relationship with the energy, warmth, and fervor that described its initial days. It is a pledge to supporting the close to home and actual connection that supports love all through the times of life. The accompanying pages will enlighten the groundbreaking force of reigniting energy and love, ability to uncover to make a relationship is alive, energetic, and profoundly satisfying.

Thus, let us set out on this extraordinary exportation together, with open hearts and receptive outlooks, prepared to embrace the lovely craft of keeping the romance alive. May this part guide you in sustaining a relationship that flourishes with enthusiasm, intimacy, and an affection that proceeds to develop and develop, filling your lives with euphoria, connection, and boundless conceivable outcomes.

In the journey of a long-lasting relationship, it's common for the initial spark and excitement to evolve over time. However, the importance of keeping the romance alive should not be underestimated. The topic of "Keeping the Romance Alive: Reigniting Passion and Love" delves into the significance of maintaining a vibrant and passionate connection with your partner and explores strategies to reignite the flame of love and passion.

Keeping the romance alive is crucial for nurturing a fulfilling and intimate partnership. It involves intentionally investing in the emotional and physical aspects of the relationship, consistently demonstrating love, affection, and appreciation for one another.

One key element in keeping the romance alive is fostering open and heartfelt communication. Partners openly express their desires, needs, and fantasies, creating an atmosphere of trust, acceptance, and vulnerability. They engage in active listening, seeking to understand and validate each other's emotions and aspirations. Through open communication, couples can explore new ways to reignite passion, address any concerns, and keep the lines of connection and understanding open.

Rekindling the physical intimacy is also vital in keeping the romance alive. Partners prioritize nurturing a fulfilling and satisfying sexual connection. They engage in open and honest discussions about their desires, fantasies, and preferences, creating an environment where both partners feel safe and comfortable expressing their needs. They make time for intimate moments, exploring new experiences, and finding ways to connect physically with affection, touch, and sensuality.

Embracing novelty and adventure is another essential aspect of keeping the romance alive. Couples actively seek new experiences and engage in activities that bring excitement and spontaneity to their relationship. They embark on adventures together, whether it's trying new hobbies, exploring new places, or engaging in shared interests. By embracing novelty, couples inject freshness and excitement into their connection, reigniting the spark of passion and adventure.

Cultivating emotional connection and nurturing the emotional intimacy between partners is paramount in keeping the romance alive. Partners create rituals of connection, such as regular date nights, deep conversations, or shared experiences that foster emotional closeness and connection. They prioritize quality time together, away from distractions, allowing for deepening emotional bonds and strengthening the emotional foundation of their relationship.

Expressing love and appreciation through gestures, both big and small, is a powerful way to keep the romance alive. Partners engage in acts of kindness, surprise gestures, and expressions of gratitude to show their love and appreciation for one another. They make an effort to notice and acknowledge the positive qualities and actions of their partner, creating an atmosphere of love and appreciation that fuels the romance.

Maintaining individuality within the relationship is also important for keeping the romance alive. Partners support and encourage each other's personal growth, interests, and passions. They allow each other space for self-expression, personal goals, and pursuits. By maintaining individuality, couples bring a sense of vitality, excitement, and intrigue to the relationship, which in turn fuels the romance and keeps the connection alive.

Taking time for self-care and prioritizing personal well-being is crucial in keeping the romance alive. Partners recognize the importance of nurturing their own happiness, fulfillment, and self-love. They engage in activities that bring them joy, invest in self-reflection and personal growth, and prioritize their physical and mental well-being. By taking care of themselves, partners bring a sense of vitality and positive energy to the relationship, creating an environment where romance can flourish.

Ultimately, keeping the romance alive requires effort, intentionality, and a genuine desire to prioritize and nurture the love and passion in the relationship. By fostering open communication, nurturing physical and emotional intimacy, embracing novelty, expressing love and appreciation, maintaining individuality, and prioritizing self-care, couples can reignite the flame of passion and love, creating a lasting and fulfilling romantic connection.

Chapter 9

Creating Shared Dreams: Setting Goals and Building a Future

A dependable relationship isn't just a festival of the present yet in addition a journey into the future, a common excursion where two spirits entwine their fantasies, desires, and dreams of what lies ahead. In this section, "Crating Shared Dreams: Setting Goals and Building a Future," we set out on an enamoring investigation of how to develop a relationship that blossoms with shared dreams, common objectives, and an aggregate vision that drives us forward as one.

As people, we frequently have our own fantasies and desires, formed by our novel encounters, interests, and wants. Notwithstanding, inside the safe-haven of a serious connection, there is a significant chance to mesh those singular dreams into an embroidery of shared dreams, making a dream that is more prominent than the amount of its parts. By adjusting our yearnings and defining objectives together, we fabricate a strong groundwork whereupon we can develop a future loaded up with reason, development, and satisfaction.

Making shared dreams isn't tied in with forfeiting uniqueness or compromising individual cravings. About finding the enchantment unfurls when two hearts thump as one, when dreams are entwined and prosper together. It is an encouragement to participate in significant discussions, to dig into the profundities of our deepest desires, and to imagine a future that lights enthusiasm, fervor, and a significant feeling of fellowship.

In this part, we will leave on a charming investigation of the components that add to making shared dreams inside a relationship. We will dig into the meaning of transparent communication, where genuine exchanges act as the compass directing us towards our aggregate vision. We will investigate the force of undivided attention, sympathy, and common understanding as fundamental fixings in cultivating a space where the two partners can share their fantasies unafraid of judgment or limit.

Besides, we will wander into the domain of objective setting, perceiving the extraordinary force of setting expectations and pursuing them collectively. We will investigate the craft of making a common guide, where achievements and accomplishments become loved snapshots of festivity and development. We will likewise talk about the significance of supporting each other's singular objectives, perceiving that sustaining individual desires upgrades the aggregate strength of the connections.

As you draw in with this part, pause for a minute to ponder your own relationship and the fantasies that dwell inside your souls. Think about the desires, objectives, and dreams that you long to show together. Consider the manners by which you can team up, support one another, and make a space where your common dreams can prosper.

Making shared dreams is a challenge to leave on an enrapturing excursion of co-creation and aggregate development. It is an affirmation that when two hearts adjust and their fantasies entwine, the conceivable outcomes become unfathomable. The accompanying pages will enlighten the extraordinary force of making shared dreams, uncovering its capacity to encourage solidarity, reason, and a steadfast bond that pushes you forward, connected at the hip, towards a future loaded up with affection, accomplishment, and shared satisfaction.

Thus, let us set out on this charming investigation together, with open hearts and receptive outlooks, prepared to embrace the significant craft of making shared dreams. May this section guide you in laying out objectives, developing an aggregate vision, and building a future that mirrors the substance of your adoration and the limitless potential that lies within your shared dreams.

In a long-lasting relationship, the act of creating shared dreams and setting goals together is a powerful way to foster a sense of purpose, unity, and growth. The topic of "Creating Shared Dreams: Setting Goals and Building a Future" explores the significance of aligning aspirations, working collaboratively, and building a shared vision for the future of a relationship.

Creating shared dreams involves actively engaging in conversations and envisioning a collective future. Partners take the time to explore their individual values, aspirations, and desires, and then merge them into a shared vision that encompasses both their personal growth and the growth of the relationship. By aligning their dreams, couples can build a foundation for a fulfilling and purpose-driven journey together.

Setting goals within the context of a shared vision provides direction, focus, and motivation for both partners. By identifying specific milestones, experiences, or achievements they want to pursue as a couple, partners create a roadmap for their future. These goals can encompass various aspects of life, such as career, family, personal development, or travel. By setting shared goals, couples create a sense of unity and collaboration, as they work together to bring their vision to life.

Building a future together involves active participation and commitment from both partners. It requires open communication, mutual support, and the willingness to adapt and grow alongside each other. As partners navigate through life's challenges and opportunities, they constantly reassess and redefine their goals, making adjustments and refinements to ensure alignment with their evolving aspirations. This continuous process of setting and revisiting goals fosters ongoing growth, resilience, and a sense of purpose in the relationship.

Shared dreams and goals serve as a driving force that propels the relationship forward. They provide motivation during challenging times and inspire both partners to push beyond their comfort zones and pursue their shared vision. When couples share dreams, they create a sense of collective identity and purpose, deepening their bond and commitment to one another.

Creating shared dreams and setting goals also encourages active collaboration and teamwork. Partners become each other's cheerleaders, supporting and challenging one another to reach their full potential. They celebrate achievements together, learn from setbacks, and inspire each other to persevere. The process of setting and pursuing shared goals strengthens the bond between partners, fostering a deep sense of trust, unity, and a shared sense of accomplishment.

The act of creating shared dreams and setting goals together also cultivates a sense of anticipation and excitement for the future. Partners have something to look forward to, to work towards, and to share in their journey. It ignites a sense of hope and optimism, enhancing the overall quality of the relationship.

Moreover, the process of setting goals and building a shared future requires effective communication and compromise. Partners learn to navigate differences, find common ground, and make decisions together. They develop negotiation skills, practice active listening, and learn to prioritize and balance individual needs and desires within the framework of the shared vision.

Ultimately, creating shared dreams and setting goals is a powerful tool for strengthening a long-lasting relationship. It provides a sense of direction, purpose, and unity, allowing partners to grow individually and as a couple. Through open communication, collaboration, and a shared commitment to their vision, couples can embark on a journey of growth, achievement, and shared fulfillment. By continuously revisiting and nurturing their shared dreams and goals, partners build a future that is meaningful, purposeful, and deeply rewarding.

Part IV

Embracing the Joys of Long-Term Love

Chapter 10

Celebrating Milestones: Honoring and Reflecting on the Journey

In the magnificent tapestry of a long-lasting relationship, there are moments that stand out like radiant stars, marking the milestones along our shared path. These milestones, both grand and subtle, represent the triumphs, challenges, and transformative experiences that have shaped our journey together. In this chapter, "Celebrating Milestones: Honoring and Reflecting on the Journey," we embark on a creative and heartfelt exploration of how to cherish and commemorate the significant moments that have woven our love story into a tapestry of memories and growth.

Milestones are the colorful brushstrokes that paint the canvas of our relationship, creating a mosaic of shared experiences, growth, and deep connection. They serve as powerful reminders of our resilience, commitment, and the depth of our love. Each milestone, whether it be an anniversary, a career achievement, a personal breakthrough, or the overcoming of a challenging time, holds within it a story worth celebrating and honoring.

Celebrating milestones is not merely an act of marking time but an opportunity to reflect on the profound journey we have undertaken together. It is a chance to pause, to cherish the moments that have shaped us, and to express gratitude for the joys and lessons we have shared. It is through celebration that we infuse our relationship with a sense of appreciation, wonder, and a deepened bond that carries us forward.

In this chapter, we embark on a creative exploration of the art of celebrating milestones within a relationship. We will delve into the significance of reflection, where we pause to honor the lessons learned, the growth achieved, and the resilience that has carried us through. We will explore the power of rituals and traditions, as they provide a sacred space to commemorate and infuse meaning into our milestones.

Furthermore, we will venture into the realm of creative expressions of celebration, recognizing that honoring milestones can take many forms. From heartfelt gestures and surprise events to shared adventures and thoughtful gifts, we will explore ways to manifest our love and appreciation for each other during these special moments.

As you engage with this chapter, take a moment to reflect on your own relationship and the milestones you have shared. Consider the moments of triumph, the challenges overcome, and the growth experienced along the way. Reflect on the ways in which you can infuse these milestones with meaning, celebrate them in unique and creative ways, and use them as stepping stones for the future.

Celebrating milestones is an invitation to bask in the radiant glow of our shared journey, to honor the transformative moments that have shaped us, and to express profound gratitude for the love and connection that have blossomed along the way. The following pages will illuminate the transformative power of celebrating milestones, revealing its ability to deepen our appreciation for each other, strengthen our bond, and create a love story that is woven with golden threads of joy, resilience, and shared accomplishment.

So, let us embark on this creative exploration together, with open hearts and open minds, ready to embrace the art of celebrating milestones. May this chapter inspire you to honor the moments that have shaped your journey, to reflect on the depths of your connection, and to infuse your relationship with a sense of wonder, gratitude, and an unwavering celebration of love.

In a long-lasting relationship, celebrating milestones plays a vital role in honoring the journey shared by partners and reflecting on the growth, accomplishments, and experiences they have encountered together. The topic of "Celebrating Milestones: Honoring and Reflecting on the Journey" explores the significance of acknowledging and commemorating important moments, both big and small, in a relationship.

Milestones serve as markers along the path of a relationship, representing significant achievements, transitions, or memorable events. These milestones can range from anniversaries and birthdays to personal achievements, such as career advancements or reaching personal goals. By consciously recognizing and celebrating these milestones, partners honor the progress they have made, the challenges they have overcome, and the growth they have experienced together.

Honoring milestones is a way of expressing gratitude and appreciation for the shared journey. Partners take the time to reflect on the memories and experiences they have accumulated, cherishing the moments of joy, love, and resilience. It is a time to acknowledge the effort, commitment, and sacrifices made along the way, recognizing the shared contributions that have shaped the relationship.

Celebrating milestones allows partners to reminisce and reconnect with the emotions and significance of past experiences. It provides an opportunity to relive special moments, revisit shared memories, and deepen the emotional connection between partners. By doing so, couples create a sense of nostalgia, fostering a deeper appreciation for the journey they have embarked on together.

Moreover, celebrating milestones strengthens the bond between partners and reinforces their commitment to one another. It serves as a reminder of the resilience and growth that has been achieved as a couple. By acknowledging the milestones, partners affirm their dedication, love, and support for each other, further solidifying the foundation of the relationship.

In addition to honoring the past, celebrating milestones also offers an opportunity to envision the future. Partners can use these moments as a springboard to set new goals, create new dreams, and explore new possibilities. It becomes a time to reflect on the lessons learned, to assess the path ahead, and to envision the next steps in the journey. By celebrating milestones, partners renew their sense of purpose and motivation to continue growing and evolving together.

The act of celebrating milestones can take various forms. It can involve intimate moments of reflection and gratitude shared between partners, or it can involve gathering loved ones to commemorate and honor the occasion. It can be a time for heartfelt conversations, exchanging meaningful gifts, or engaging in special activities that hold significance for the relationship. The key is to tailor the celebration to the unique dynamics and preferences of the couple, ensuring that it truly reflects their journey and the values they hold dear.

By regularly celebrating milestones, partners infuse their relationship with positivity, appreciation, and a sense of accomplishment. It reinforces the foundation of love and strengthens the emotional connection between partners. It serves as a reminder of the joys and triumphs they have experienced together, fostering a deep sense of gratitude and fulfillment.

All in all, celebrating milestones is a powerful way to honor and reflect on the journey shared by partners in a long-lasting relationship. It serves as a reminder of the growth, resilience, and accomplishments achieved together. By acknowledging these milestones, partners deepen their connection, renew their commitment, and foster an environment of love, appreciation, and shared aspirations. It is a beautiful opportunity to pause, reflect, and celebrate the extraordinary journey they continue to embark on together.

Chapter 11

Nurturing Friendship: The Role of Companionship in a Lasting Relationship

In the embroidery of a durable relationship, companionship fills in as the tough string that winds around two hearts together. It is the establishment whereupon love blooms and twists, making a profound feeling of friendship, trust, and understanding. In this section, "Nurturing Friendship: The Role of Companionship in a Lasting Relationship," we set out on a genuine investigation of how developing and valuing the fellowship inside our connection can reinforce the powers of profound devotion, cultivate common help, and make a deep rooted association that goes the distance.

Friendship is the captivating orchestra that reverberates inside the center of our relationship. A bond rises above the heartfelt association, permitting us to track down comfort, giggling, and a feeling of straightforwardness in one another's presence. It is through friendship hat we become each other's comrades, partners, and team promoters, making a place of refuge where weakness and realness flourish.

Sustaining companionship inside an enduring relationship isn't about just coinciding or depending entirely on the heartfelt parts of affection. It is tied in with embracing each other as companions and sidekicks, praising the common interests, interests, and experiences that make our bond novel. It is an encouragement to cultivate a profound feeling of brotherhood, where we can be our actual selves, track down satisfaction in one another's connection, and make recollections that entwine our lives.

In this section, we leave on a genuine investigation of the job of kinship in an enduring relationship. We will dive into the meaning of open correspondence, where we share our considerations, dreams, and fears with a feeling of trust and weakness. We will investigate the force of chuckling and happiness, perceiving that common snapshots of euphoria and perkiness are the underpinning areas of strength for a strong friendship.

Moreover, we will wander into the domain of shared encounters, recognizing the extraordinary force of making recollections together. From leaving on new undertakings and seeking after normal leisure activities to taking part in profound discussions and supporting each other's singular development, we will investigate ways of sustaining the fellowship that underlies our affection.

As you draw in with this part, pause for a minute to ponder the fellowship inside your own relationship. Think about the snapshots of giggling, understanding, and relentless help that have molded your bond. Ponder the manners by which you can cultivate and esteem this fellowship, injecting it with aim, care, and a profound appreciation for one another's novel characteristics.

Sustaining friendships inside an enduring relationship is an encouragement to develop a profound feeling of association, understanding, and friendship. An affirmation of genuine affection flourishes when it is grounded in the groundwork of companionship. The accompanying pages will enlighten the groundbreaking force of sustaining kinship, uncovering the skill to make a relationship based on trust, validity, and a significant feeling of friendship.

Thus, let us leave on this ardent investigation together, with open hearts and receptive outlooks, prepared to embrace the specialty of supporting kinship. May this section motivate you to develop the obligation of companionship inside your relationship, to esteem the snapshots of giggling and association, and to make an organization that isn't just based on adoration however on the getting through strength of a valid and enduring friendship.

Friendship is often considered the foundation of a strong and lasting romantic relationship. The topic of "Nurturing Friendship: The Role of Companionship in a Lasting Relationship" explores the significance of cultivating a deep and meaningful friendship between partners and how it contributes to the longevity and happiness of their relationship.

In a lasting relationship, companionship goes beyond the romantic aspects and encompasses a genuine and authentic friendship. Nurturing friendship involves building a strong bond of trust, mutual respect, and support between partners. It is about being each other's confidants, allies, and companions through the ups and downs of life.

The role of companionship in a lasting relationship is multifaceted. Firstly, a strong friendship between partners creates a sense of emotional security and comfort. It provides a safe space where partners can be themselves, without fear of judgment or rejection. They can share their joys, sorrows, dreams, and fears with one another, knowing that they will be met with understanding and empathy. This emotional support and connection fostered through friendship strengthens the overall foundation of the relationship.

Nurturing friendship also involves engaging in shared interests and activities. Partners find joy in spending quality time together, exploring common hobbies, and creating lasting memories. They genuinely enjoy each other's company and prioritize the time they spend together. By actively participating in shared experiences, partners deepen their bond, create a sense of togetherness, and foster a sense of adventure and excitement in their relationship.

Furthermore, friendship in a lasting relationship involves open and honest communication. Partners are not only romantic partners but also effective communicators. They engage in meaningful conversations, actively listen to one another, and communicate their needs, desires, and concerns. This open and honest dialogue allows partners to understand each other on a deeper level and find mutually satisfying solutions to any conflicts or challenges they may face.

Companionship also plays a vital role in supporting personal growth and development within the relationship. True friends uplift and inspire each other to become the best versions of themselves. In a lasting relationship, partners support one another's aspirations, encourage personal growth, and celebrate individual achievements. They become each other's cheerleaders, providing a source of motivation, encouragement, and accountability.

Moreover, the role of companionship in a lasting relationship is closely tied to shared values and a shared vision for the future. True friends align their goals, dreams, and values, creating a strong sense of unity and purpose. They collaborate in making important decisions, taking into account each other's perspectives and desires. By nurturing friendship, partners foster a strong sense of teamwork and partnership, allowing them to navigate life's challenges and celebrate successes together.

In a lasting relationship, nurturing friendship is an ongoing process that requires effort, time, and commitment from both partners. It involves continuously investing in the emotional connection, creating shared experiences, and practicing active listening and understanding. Partners must prioritize friendship as an integral part of their relationship, ensuring that it remains vibrant and strong.

At last, nurturing friendship in a lasting relationship is essential for creating a deep, meaningful, and fulfilling connection between partners. It forms the foundation of trust, support, and companionship that sustains the relationship through various seasons of life. By cultivating a strong friendship, partners not only strengthen their romantic bond but also create a lifelong partnership built on trust, respect, and genuine love.

Chapter 12

Savoring Everyday Moments: Finding Joy in the Simplest Things

In the fast-paced world we live in, it's easy to get caught up in the demands of our daily lives and overlook the beauty and joy that exists in the simplest of moments. Yet, within these seemingly mundane instances lies a treasure trove of happiness, connection, and fulfillment waiting to be discovered. In this extensive exploration of "Savoring Everyday Moments: Finding Joy in the Simplest Things," we embark on a transformative journey that invites us to slow down, embrace the present, and infuse our lives and relationships with a profound sense of wonder, gratitude, and joy.

Life is a tapestry woven with countless threads, and it is often the subtlest of details that add the most vibrant colors to our existence. Savoring everyday moments is about cultivating a mindful awareness, a conscious choice to be fully present and engage with the beauty that surrounds us. It is an invitation to celebrate the ordinary and discover the extraordinary within it.

When we savor everyday moments, we awaken our senses to the richness of life. We learn to appreciate the warmth of a morning sunbeam gently caressing our skin, the soothing aroma of a freshly brewed cup of coffee, the soft melody of raindrops dancing on the windowpane. It is in these seemingly small moments that we find solace, inspiration, and a deep connection to the world and the people we cherish.

In this extensive exploration, we embark on a journey of self-discovery and relationship enrichment. We delve into the transformative power of mindfulness, learning to cultivate an open-hearted presence that allows us to fully experience and appreciate each passing moment. We explore the art of gratitude, recognizing that by acknowledging and cherishing the simplest blessings in our lives, we invite more joy and abundance into our days.

Moreover, we recognize that savoring everyday moments is not a solitary endeavor. It is a shared experience, a beautiful opportunity to deepen our connections with loved ones. We explore the importance of quality time and meaningful conversations, creating space for authentic connections and heartfelt exchanges. We learn to create rituals and traditions that celebrate the ordinary, infusing our relationships with a sense of joy, meaning, and a lasting bond.

As you engage with this extensive exploration, take a moment to reflect on the everyday moments that have shaped your own journey. Recall the laughter shared over a meal, the feeling of a loved one's embrace, the serenity of a quiet evening stroll. Contemplate the beauty that surrounds you, waiting to be discovered and savored.

Savoring everyday moments is an invitation to live fully, to awaken to the magic that exists in the simplest of things. It is a conscious choice to slow down, to embrace the present, and to nurture a deep appreciation for the intricacies of life. The following pages will guide you through an extensive exploration of savoring everyday moments, offering insights, practices, and inspiration to infuse your life and relationships with joy, gratitude, and a profound sense of connection.

So, let us embark on this transformative journey together, with open hearts and curious minds, ready to savor the beauty that unfolds in the simplest of moments. May this extensive exploration inspire you to pause, to breathe, and to cultivate a deep sense of joy and gratitude as you savor the everyday moments that weave the tapestry of your life.

The topic of "Savoring Everyday Moments: Finding Joy in the Simplest Things" explores the transformative practice of appreciating and finding joy in the ordinary moments of life. It recognizes that amidst the hustle and bustle of daily routines, there are countless opportunities to experience profound happiness and fulfillment by simply being present and mindful of the simplest things.

The extensive exploration aims to shed light on the power of savoring and cultivating gratitude for the small, often overlooked moments that make up our lives. It emphasizes that true joy and contentment can be found not in grand gestures or extraordinary events but in the beauty and significance of everyday experiences.

Savoring refers to the intentional act of fully immersing oneself in the present moment, engaging all the senses and experiencing a deep appreciation for what is happening in the here and now. It involves slowing down, observing the details, and embracing a sense of wonder and gratitude for the seemingly mundane aspects of life.

Finding joy in the simplest things is an invitation to shift our perspective and cultivate a mindset of gratitude and positivity. It encourages us to pause and reflect on the small pleasures that bring us happiness, whether it be savoring a cup of coffee in the morning, enjoying a walk in nature, or sharing a heartfelt conversation with a loved one.

The exploration highlights the transformative impact of savoring everyday moments on our overall well-being. By consciously directing our attention to the present moment and finding joy in the simplest things, we enhance our ability to experience happiness, reduce stress, and cultivate a greater sense of fulfillment in our lives.

It also emphasizes the importance of mindfulness as a tool for savoring everyday moments. Mindfulness involves being fully present, non-judgmentally aware of our thoughts, feelings, and sensations. By practicing mindfulness, we can cultivate a deeper connection to the present moment and develop a heightened awareness of the beauty and significance of ordinary experiences.

The exploration offers practical strategies, mindfulness exercises, and insights to inspire individuals to incorporate the practice of savoring into their daily lives. It encourages individuals to cultivate a sense of curiosity, appreciation, and gratitude for the small moments that often go unnoticed but hold immense potential for joy and fulfillment.

Ultimately, the exploration aims to inspire individuals to embrace the practice of savoring everyday moments, recognizing that true happiness can be found in the simplest things. It invites us to shift our focus from chasing grand achievements to cultivating a deep appreciation for the richness and beauty of the present moment, leading to a more joyful, meaningful, and fulfilling life.

Conclusion

Embracing the Gift of a Long-Lasting Relationship

In this extensive exploration of navigating the joys and challenges of a long-lasting relationship, we have embarked on a transformative journey of love, growth, and connection. Through the exploration of various themes such as trust, communication, individuality, emotional intimacy, conflict resolution, support, continuous growth, romance, shared dreams, and celebrating milestones, we have gained valuable insights and practical tools to foster a strong and fulfilling partnership.

As we conclude this exploration, it is important to reflect on the profound gift that a long-lasting relationship offers. A long-lasting relationship is not merely a stroke of luck or chance; it is a testament to the commitment, dedication, and hard work invested by both partners. It is a testament to the depth of love and the strength of the bond that has weathered the storms and celebrated the triumphs.

Embracing the gift of a long-lasting relationship means cherishing the journey that you have traveled together. It means recognizing and appreciating the growth and transformation that both individuals have undergone, individually and as a couple. It involves acknowledging the challenges faced and the lessons learned, and integrating them into the fabric of your shared story.

Embracing the gift of a long-lasting relationship also means remaining present and engaged in the present moment. It involves continuing to nurture the connection, love, and intimacy that brought you together in the first place. It means valuing and savoring the small moments, as well as the grand ones, and finding joy in the everyday experiences shared.

Furthermore, embracing the gift of a long-lasting relationship necessitates an ongoing commitment to growth and continuous improvement. It means recognizing that a relationship is a living entity that requires attention, care, and effort. It involves actively seeking new ways to deepen the emotional bond, explore shared interests, and support each other's individual dreams and aspirations.

In conclusion, embracing the gift of a long-lasting relationship is an invitation to appreciate the beauty, depth, and resilience that a committed partnership can bring. It is an acknowledgment of the unique journey that you and your partner have embarked upon, with all its highs and lows. It is a celebration of the love, connection, and shared experiences that have shaped your lives together.

As you continue on your path, may you carry the lessons and insights from this exploration in your hearts. May you embrace the challenges as opportunities for growth, and may you nurture the love and connection that form the foundation of your long-lasting relationship. Remember that the gift of a long-lasting relationship is a precious one, worthy of celebration, gratitude, and continual investment.

May your journey be filled with an abundance of love, joy, and fulfillment as you navigate the beautiful path of a long-lasting relationship together.